To ~~~~~~~~~~
fun – Love
Aunt Vol.
6/17/04

around

WASHINGTON D.C., with KIDS

by Kathryn McKay

3rd EDITION

FODOR'S TRAVEL PUBLICATIONS

New York ✳ Toronto ✳ London ✳ Sydney ✳ Auckland

www.fodors.com

CREDITS

Writer: Kathryn McKay

Series Editors: Karen Cure, Andrea Lehman
Editor: Diane Mehta
Editorial Production: Ira-Neil Dittersdorf, Kristin Milavec
Production/Manufacturing: Robert B. Shields

Design: Fabrizio La Rocca, *creative director;*
Tigist Getachew, *art director*
Cover Art and Design: Jessie Hartland
Flip Art and Illustration: Rico Lins, Keren Ora Admoni/Rico Lins Studio

ABOUT THE WRITER
Each month writer Kathryn McKay scours the D.C. area with her two children in tow researching her column, "In Our Own Backyard," for *Washington Parent* magazine.

Third Edition
ISBN 1–4000–1365–8
ISSN 1526–1980

IMPORTANT TIP
Although all prices, opening times, and other details in this book are based on information supplied to us at press time, changes occur all the time in the travel world, and Fodor's cannot accept responsibility for facts that become outdated or for inadvertent errors or omissions. So always confirm information when it matters, especially if you're making a detour to visit a specific place.

SPECIAL SALES
Fodor's Travel Publications are available at special discounts for bulk purchases for sales promotions or premiums. Special editions, including personalized covers, excerpts of existing guides, and corporate imprints, can be created in large quantities for special needs. For more information, contact your local bookseller or Special Markets, Fodor's Travel Publications, 1745 Broadway, New York, NY 10019. Inquiries from Canada should be directed to your local Canadian bookseller or sent to Random House of Canada, Ltd., Marketing Dept., 2775 Matheson Boulevard East, Mississauga, Ontario L4W 4P7. Inquiries from the United Kingdom should be sent to Fodor's Travel Publications, 20 Vauxhall Bridge Road, London, England SW1V 2SA.

PRINTED IN THE UNITED STATES OF AMERICA
10 9 8 7 6 5 4 3 2 1

COUNTDOWN TO GOOD TIMES

GET READY, GET SET!

What child wouldn't be excited to touch a moon rock, see Dorothy's ruby slippers, or cruise along the C&O Canal in a canal barge pulled by mules? Washington may seem like a place that's mainly for grown-ups and school trips. After all, running the government of a superpower is serious stuff. But the city of the White House and the Capitol is also home to the Capital Children's Museum, the National Museum of Natural History, and the National Zoo. History that seems dry and dusty in the classroom comes alive for children as they visit landmarks they've seen in movies and on TV, ride horses through the same park where presidents have ridden, and watch thousands of dollars roll off the presses at the Bureau of Engraving and Printing. A big plus in Washington is that most attractions are free.

GET PREPARED

You could just take the Metro to the Smithsonian stop, get off at the National Mall, and wander around. And you'd probably have fun.

Or you can prepare yourself and your children. Flip through this book. The first time, flip through fast, and check out Abe Lincoln and his admirers in the lower right corner. Next, take the time to read the listings, and use the directories in the back of the book to find just what you're looking for. Last but not least, bring this book with you as you explore. It'll help you get even more out of your visits.

Before you leave, call for information—especially if you go on a holiday (when Washington is generally very crowded). The hours listed in this book are the usual operating hours. Some places are open longer or shorter or not at all on holidays, and fees and hours are always subject to change. For those sights that do charge admission, we list only the regular adult, student (with ID), and kids' prices; children under the ages specified are free. In addition, some discounts are offered for families or for a particular status or affiliation; it never hurts to ask.

To find current kids' activities and events going on in and around the city, look in the "Friday Weekend" section of the *Washington Post* and in *Washington Parent,* a monthly publication available free at libraries and many grocery stores.

GET AROUND

For train lovers, riding Washington's Metro (subway) system can be as thrilling as exploring your destination. But before you go, remember that Metro stations don't have public rest rooms. Buy your ticket at the Farecard machines, or better yet, let your kids put their math minds to work and put the money in the machines. The base fare is $1.20; the actual price you pay depends on the time of day and distance traveled. Children 4 and under ride free. But after you go through the turnstiles to enter, consider collecting your kids' cards. You'll need them again to exit.

Each line of the Metrorail is color coded: red, orange, blue, green, and yellow. You can move from one line to another at transfer stations. As a precaution, be sure shoelaces are tied and scarves are tucked in before you ride Metro escalators, some of which are more than 200 feet long. If your children are afraid of heights or you have a little one in a stroller, take the elevators. All the stations have them, though about a third of them are across the street from Metro entrances.

If, on the other hand, you decide to navigate behind the wheel, it's relatively easy to get your bearings in this diamond-shape city. With the Capitol as its hub, Washington is composed of four quadrants—Northwest (NW), Northeast (NE), Southwest (SW), and Southeast (SE)—divided by North, South, and East Capitol streets and, on the west side of the Capitol, by the National Mall instead of a street. Within each of these quadrants, the roads running north and south are numbered, and east to west roads are named after letters of the alphabet. (You won't find an A or B street because A Street became the Mall and East Capitol Street and B Street was renamed Constitution Avenue to the north and Independence Avenue to the south.) After the lettered streets come longer street names in alphabetical order, and the alphabetical lineup repeats itself until the Maryland and Virginia borders. Add to the mix a number of diagonal avenues named for states, the most prominent being Massachusetts, Connecticut, and Pennsylvania avenues. Traffic circles and one-way streets can add to the confusion for adults but can be fun for kids, who can look for the statues and fountains in the centers of the circles.

Around the outskirts, the Capital beltway girds Washington like—you guessed it—a big belt. If you do go downtown, keep in mind that parking may be limited and expensive, especially during the week. For most suburban sights, parking is free and plentiful.

GET ORIENTED

When you arrive at a sight, be prepared to walk through metal detectors and open your bags for security personnel. Visit the information desk for maps and brochures, and inquire about children's programs. Also, show your kids how to recognize staff or security people, and designate a time and place—some visible landmark—to meet in case you become separated. It goes without saying that you should keep an eye on your children at all times, especially if they are small.

GET GOING

Finally, after you've planned and scheduled and traveled, have fun. And try to be as spontaneous as your children.

GET IN TOUCH

We'd love to hear from you. What did you and your children think about the places we recommend? Have you found other places we should include? Send us your ideas via e-mail (c/o editors@fodors.com, specifying *Around Washington, D.C. with Kids* on the subject line) or snail mail (c/o Around Washington, D.C. with Kids, Fodor's Travel Publications, 1745 Broadway, New York, NY 10019). In the meantime, get ready, get set, and go have a great time seeing Washington, D.C., with your kids!

—Kathryn McKay

ARLINGTON NATIONAL CEMETERY

68

Don't be surprised if your children click their heels together for a while after watching the changing of the guard at the Tomb of the Unknowns. Here soldiers from the Army's 3rd U.S. Infantry Regiment (Old Guard) keep watch 24 hours a day, regardless of weather. Each sentinel marches 21 steps (children can count them silently), clicks his or her heels, and faces the tomb for 21 seconds, symbolizing the 21-gun salute—all while carrying an M-14 rifle weighing 10 pounds. The changing of the guard is a precise ceremony, held every half hour during the day from April through September and every hour the rest of the year. (At night, when the cemetery's closed, it's every two hours.)

Kids may also be interested in famous grave sites. Some 285,000 American war dead and many notable Americans are interred in these 625 acres. John F. Kennedy is buried under an eternal flame near two of his children, who died in infancy, and his wife, Jacqueline Bouvier Kennedy Onassis. His is the most visited grave in the country. Nearby, a simple white cross marks the resting place of his brother Robert. William Howard Taft, 27th president

GETTING THERE You can ride the Metro, take a Tourmobile bus (tel. 202/554–7950), walk across Memorial Bridge (southwest of the Lincoln Memorial), or drive. There's a large paid parking lot at the skylit visitor center on Memorial Drive. Only those with a family member buried here (and a vehicle pass) can drive within the cemetery. Others must tour on foot, which means a fair bit of hiking, but also up-close looks at the graves. To reach Ft. Myer, take U.S. 50 west to the Iwo Jima Memorial exit. Stay straight to enter the Wright Gate. MPs will provide directions to the stables.

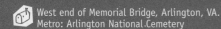
West end of Memorial Bridge, Arlington, VA.
Metro: Arlington National Cemetery

Free

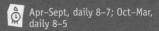
Apr–Sept, daily 8–7; Oct–Mar, daily 8–5

703/607–8052, 703/697–2131 for specific grave; www.arlingtoncemetery.org

6 and up

and Supreme Court justice, lies here, as do famous veterans Joe Louis (boxer), Lee Marvin (actor), and Abner Doubleday (reputed inventor of baseball). A memorial to the Space Shuttle *Challenger* is here, too.

While at Arlington, you will probably hear the clear, doleful sound of a bugler playing taps or the sharp reports of a gun salute. On average, 25 funerals are held here daily. You'll want to remind your child that this is sacred ground; respect and quiet are always necessary.

If you're driving and have an extra 30–60 minutes, consider taking a free tour of the stables at nearby Ft. Myer (Arlington Blvd. [U.S. 50], tel. 703/696–3147), operated by the Old Guard's Caisson Platoon and open 12–4. Kids can bring carrots or apples to feed the horses, who participate in funerals at Arlington, weddings at Ft. Myer, and parades throughout D.C.

EATS FOR KIDS
No food or drink is allowed at the cemetery. In Arlington, **Queen Bee** (3181 Wilson Blvd., tel. 703/527–3444) is a superb Vietnamese restaurant; for all-American barbecue, try **Red Hot & Blue** (1600 Wilson Blvd., tel. 703/276–7427). For suggestions in Washington, see the DAR Museum and the White House.

HEY, KIDS! Check out the grave of the Drummer Boy of Chickamauga (a Civil War battle). John Lincoln Clem was 9 years old when he was a drummer boy and 12 when he became an active-duty soldier—the youngest ever in the U.S. Army! He eventually retired as a major general in 1916. Clem fought for the Union, but both Union and Confederate soldiers are buried at Arlington.

AUDUBON NATURALIST
SOCIETY'S WOODEND

Don't let bad weather keep the kids inside. In fact, no matter what it's like outside, there'll be something interesting to see and do at this nature sanctuary. Snow and mud make finding animal tracks easier as you play nature detective. On hot, humid days, crickets form a chorus with cicadas, and butterflies dance in wildflower meadows. On cool, crisp fall days, you can see varied leaf colors reflected in the large pond. But on any day, you'll hear the trill of birdsong, because the Audubon Naturalist Society (ANS) has turned the grounds into something of a private nature preserve, forbidding toxic chemicals and leaving some areas in their wild, natural state.

A self-guided nature trail winds through this verdant 40-acre estate and around the local ANS's suburban Maryland headquarters. The estate is known as Woodend, as is the mansion, which was designed in the 1920s by Jefferson Memorial architect John Russell Pope. Allowing time to marvel at Mother Nature, you can complete the ¾-mile trail in about one hour. Parents of babies should use a backpack rather than a stroller, as most of the trail has wood chips.

HEY, KIDS!
Along the nature trail, you'll see not only birdhouses and bird feeders, but also houses for flying squirrels. You can learn more about these cool creatures at an Audubon Naturalist Society flying squirrel program, held periodically throughout the year.

EATS FOR KIDS Picnicking isn't allowed at Woodend without a permit, but 3 miles west, in downtown Bethesda, you can nibble your way around the world at any of 180 restaurants. **Oodles Noodles** (4907 Cordell Ave., tel. 301/986–8833) offers some of the area's best Asian cooking and best bargains. Friendly, quick service and red chili-pepper lights swooping across the ceiling make **California Tortilla** (4862 Cordell Ave., tel. 301/654–8226) a favorite for families. For a dining guide call the Bethesda Urban Partnership at 301/215–6660.

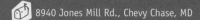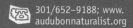

8940 Jones Mill Rd., Chevy Chase, MD

Free; family programs $5–$10, camps $195–$260

Daily sunrise–sunset; bookshop M–F 10–5, Sa 9–5, Su 12–5

301/652–9188; www. audubonnaturalist.org

3–9

For a break from the outdoors (but not the heat—the mansion isn't air-conditioned), ask at the Woodend office if you can see the library. Along with books for adults, it contains hundreds of stuffed American birds. The mansion isn't always open to the public, however, as it's rented for weddings, bar mitzvahs, and other celebrations.

During family programs (which include parents), classes, and one- to two-week camps, educated naturalists from the society's staff foster environmental awareness and unlock nature's mysteries. Each program focuses on a nature-oriented theme, like meadow habitats, pond life, or "metamorphosis magic," and includes such hands-on activities as catching insects, fishing for pond creatures with nets, or investigating rotting log communities. ANS fairs in May and December attract thousands. While you shop at the crafts show, your children can enjoy animal demonstrations and kiddie crafts. There really is lots going on here year-round.

KEEP IN MIND Please remind your kids that you can't take it with you. Every stick, leaf, rock, and insect needs to stay at Woodend. If your little collectors are disappointed by this rule, you can visit the bookshop. It sells neat souvenirs for young naturalists, including nature books, puzzles, T-shirts, and games.

BOWIE BAYSOX BASEBALL

Minor league baseball offers major league fun for young fans of the Bowie Baysox, a Class AA Eastern League affiliate of the Baltimore Orioles. Not only can you see what's happening better at the 10,000-seat Prince George's Stadium than at 50,000-seat, major-league ballparks, but you'll find as much action off the field as there is on it.

As a Baysox player slides into base, your children can slip down the slide at the playground. As players circle the diamond, your kids can circle on a carousel, which runs during the entire game, except while the national anthem plays. Little hurlers test their throwing arms in pitch-speed games.

Meanwhile, collectors spread out baseball cards in the ample bleachers, and there's plenty of room for teenagers to move a few seats away and pretend they're not really with Mom or Dad. When the ballpark is crowded, fans get more boisterous, which is also part of the entertainment. Giveaways and games throughout the summer can yield such precious kid

KEEP IN MIND Two Class A minor league teams also play in Washington's out-field: the Frederick Keys (tel. 877/846–5397) in Frederick County, Maryland, and the Cannons (tel. 703/590–2311) in Prince William County, Virginia. The Bowie stadium is newer and a little larger, and since the Baysox are Class AA, the quality of play is a little better. Otherwise the experience is much the same. Based on where you live or where you're visiting, you may want to try one of the others.

Prince George's Stadium, 4101 N.E. Crain Hwy.
(U.S. 301), Bowie, MD

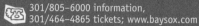 301/805–6000 information,
301/464–4865 tickets; www.baysox.com

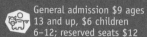 General admission $9 ages
13 and up, $6 children
6–12; reserved seats $12

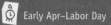 Early Apr–Labor Day

 4 and up

keepsakes as caps, jerseys, and mugs. On Saturday nights, holidays, and occasional weeknights, post-game fireworks light up the sky.

Of course, if your kids are actually interested in the game itself, they can keep track of it on electronic scoreboards and a large screen that shows replays from the field and fans in the stands. (So smile! You may be on camera.) And if they come wearing their youth athletic uniforms, they'll get in free, Sundays through Thursdays. All the activity makes minor league baseball and children a natural double-play combination. The only real downside is that your family won't see today's superstar . . . but you might see tomorrow's!

HEY, KIDS! Do you want players' autographs? It's easier to get them here than at major league stadiums. Baysox officials recommend arriving an hour and a half before the game to catch players between warm-ups and game time. Several players move up to the majors each year, so you never know whose signature you'll get.

EATS FOR KIDS At the **Kids' Stand,** peanut butter sandwiches, juice, and such typical baseball fare as hot dogs cost $1 each. (Sorry, the Kids' Stand is just for kids!) Adults pay a little more at the concession stands but get more choices. You can eat pub-type fare while watching the game from the **Diamond View** restaurant, when it's open. On most weekends and some weekdays it's booked for parties.

BUREAU OF ENGRAVING AND PRINTING

how me the money! It's here—some $637 million printed daily—and any youngster who gets an allowance will enjoy watching as bills roll off the presses. Despite the lack of free samples, the self-guided, 35-minute bureau tour is one of the city's most popular attractions. Videos and staff stationed along the tour provide explanations and background information on the printing process.

The United States began printing paper currency in 1862 to finance the Civil War and because there was a coin shortage. Two men and four women separated and sealed by hand $1 and $2 U.S. notes printed by private companies. Today, the bureau employs approximately 2,500 people, who work out of two buildings: this one and one in Fort Worth, Texas.

On tour, your children can look through wide windows to see three steps in the money-making process. First, both sides of the bills are printed in large 32-note sheets—back side first. (Bureau employees refer to bills as "notes.") Second, machines and employees

EATS FOR KIDS A healthful meal doesn't cost much at the **U.S. Department of Agriculture cafeteria** (14th St. and Independence Ave. SW, tel. 202/488–7279). Show identification and get visitor stickers at the front desk, and then choose from 10 food stations and a buffet.

KEEP IN MIND March–September, required same-day timed-entry tickets are issued starting at 8 at the Raoul Wallenberg Place SW entrance. Waits to get in can be two hours, and if a tour bus arrives as you do, you may also have to wait for tickets. While waiting outside, examine some money with your kids. Once inside, video monitors with trivia questions help pass time. For example: If you spent $1 every second, it would take 317 years to spend $10 billion. A mile-high stack of currency would contain over 14½ million notes.

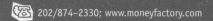 14th and C Sts. SW. Metro: Smithsonian
(Independence Ave. exit)

 Free

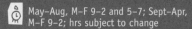 May–Aug, M–F 9–2 and 5–7; Sept–Apr,
M–F 9–2; hrs subject to change

202/874–2330; www.moneyfactory.com

 6 and up

inspect the notes for defects. For example, if a sheet was folded instead of flat during the process, the notes may only be half printed. Rejects are shredded, recycled, or sold. In the final area, serial numbers and Federal Reserve seals are printed, and the notes are cut.

Each $1 note costs 4¢–5.2¢ to print. Larger denominations cost a little extra because of security enhancements such as watermarks, color-shifting ink, and security threads. Hold one of these bills up to the light to see the vertically embedded threads. Environmentally minded kids will be glad to know that no trees are cut down to make paper currency; it's made of 75% cotton and 25% linen.

It may sound crazy to adults, but kids like to buy bags of shredded money in the bureau's gift shop. A small bag costing $1.50 contains $150 worth of bills that didn't pass inspection. For $5 your children can get slightly more practical mementos: postcards that look like currency with their photos on them.

HEY, KIDS! Would you like to make money? Ten-year-old Emma Brown did. She was the youngest employee in bureau history, but she didn't work here for the fun of it. Emma's brother, the family breadwinner, was killed in action during the Civil War, leaving Emma to care for her disabled mother and the rest of the family. Emma's congressman gave her a political appointment so she could make money by making money.

C&O CANAL NATIONAL HISTORICAL
PARK'S BOAT RIDES

64

W hen you hear the horn blow, boarding time is near. Your family can take a leisurely, mule-drawn barge ride through the lock, down the Chesapeake & Ohio (C&O) Canal, and back again. Although you won't go far physically—less than a mile—you can travel all the way back to the 1800s in your mind while costumed guides teach you about canal life. Interestingly, the C&O goes to neither the Chesapeake nor the Ohio. The Baltimore & Ohio (B&O) Railroad beat the canal to the Ohio River, and the railroad's success eventually put the canal out of business. Ironically, construction of both the C&O and B&O began on the same day, July 4, 1828. When canal construction ended in 1850, there were 74 lift-locks stretching from downtown D.C. to Cumberland, Maryland. Nevertheless, for a time the canal did prove to be economical for traders moving goods, especially coal, to the port of Georgetown, from which ships traveled to the lower Chesapeake and the Atlantic Ocean.

Most children are fascinated by the canal barge's engines: Four mules named Ada, Frances, Katie, and Rhody take turns pulling the 12-foot-wide barge along the towpath. As it passes

KEEP IN MIND Across M Street is the oldest building in Washington: the Old Stone House (3051 M St. NW, tel. 202/426–6851), built in 1764. Here five rooms are furnished with simple, sturdy artifacts of 18th-century middle-class life, but your kids might head for the garden in back, perfect for a picnic or quick game of tag. Admission is free, and the house is open Wednesday–Sunday 12–5. Teenagers might prefer Georgetown's funky boutiques.

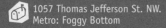
1057 Thomas Jefferson St. NW.
Metro: Foggy Bottom

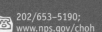
202/653–5190;
www.nps.gov/choh

$8 ages 15 and up,
$5 children 4–14

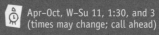
Apr–Oct, W–Su 11, 1:30, and 3
(times may change; call ahead)

3 and up

under the 15-foot-wide bridge at Thomas Jefferson Street, it may only be a canal worker's foot keeping the boat from hitting the bridge.

Don't be alarmed if your guide jumps off the boat to help with the lines and puts a child in charge for a few minutes. Said child will probably take possession of the horn and may even wear a captain's hat to make sure passengers stay in line. Eventually the guide will come back. Amid tales of canal life, he or she may treat you to some music and a few jokes. One example: "Along the canal, you may notice moss on the sides of the lock. Can you guess the name of the bird that uses the moss for its nest? The lock moss nester!" The rest of the ride should be all downhill.

EATS FOR KIDS
Drop anchor at **Washington Harbour** (3000 K St. NW, tel. 202/295–5000), a complex of condos, offices, and restaurants. Stroll the waterfront with yogurt from **TCBY** (tel. 202/298–6757), or munch popcorn shrimp from **Tony and Joe's** (tel. 202/944–4545) while watching seagulls soar, looking for their own food.

HEY, KIDS! Mules, the offspring of horses and donkeys, were chosen to pull barges because of their strength and heat tolerance and because they don't require as much hay and grain as horses. To be a true mule, your mom has to be a horse and your dad a donkey. If your father's a stallion and your mother's a donkey, you're a hinny. To remember which is which, recite this simple alliteration: The mother of the mule is the mare.

CAPITAL CHILDREN'S MUSEUM

Looking for a capital kid's adventure? You may find this rambling hands-on museum behind Union Station quirky, but for children it's fun, festive, and flooded with opportunities for exploration. The eclectic assortment of exhibits is about as organized as the contents of most kids' backpacks after they've been dumped on the floor. The museum was designed that way to encourage kids to go up and down and back and forth over three floors of exhibits. It works!

In the popular Cityscapes exhibit, your children can "drive" a Metro bus, whiz down a fire pole, and wander through the sewer system. Budding artists can create cartoons in the animation exhibit. In the Chemical Science Center, museum scientists mix chemistry with comedy to educate and entertain kids with zany experiments, including blowing up gummy bears, removing the iron from breakfast cereal, and electrocuting a pickle. In the center's lab, kids over 6 don white coats and goggles to create their own slime, learn what makes diapers absorbent, or isolate vitamin C from fruit drinks.

HEY, KIDS!
On the first floor, wave your hand over the holes in the electric harp to hear a guitar, a saxophone, an organ, and more instruments. In the second-floor bubble room, make a bubble large enough to hold you and a parent. Then pop it! On the third floor, try to find the 7,000 paper cranes made by kids from Japan after 9/11.

KEEP IN MIND
Late afternoons (nap times) tend to be the least crowded here. Whenever you come, though, allow at least three hours for exploring this huge children's paradise. Keep an eye on your kids; there are lots of staircases and elevators, plus a cave. Also, bring a backpack or large purse to carry your children's crafts. A tissue-paper flower won't be the same after being stuck in a pocket.

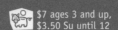
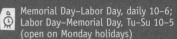

800 3rd St. NE. Metro: Union Station

$7 ages 3 and up, $3.50 Su until 12

Memorial Day–Labor Day, daily 10–6; Labor Day–Memorial Day, Tu–Su 10–5 (open on Monday holidays)

202/675–4120; www.ccm.org

1–12

Two of the larger exhibits focus on other cultures. In the Mexico exhibit, your kids can sample hot chocolate, make native crafts, climb up an Inca pyramid, and take off their shoes to enjoy a sandbox by the shore. In the Japan exhibit, they can check out kimonos and electronics in a shopping district and pretend to be students in a Japanese classroom. Changing exhibits often feature children's literature from around the world.

In the puppet room, rocking chairs for nursing mothers and hand puppets for children make a welcome combination. Special events are held on weekends and holidays throughout the year, and story hours, theme days, and puppet shows in the large auditorium enhance the museum experience. When you've finally had enough of all those hands-on experiences, pause at the museum art gallery, near the exit, where you can unwind and simply look, for a change.

EATS FOR KIDS Picnic tables can be found on the grounds and in a lunchroom with vending machines on the first floor. For heartier fare, you'll find restaurants and more than 35 food stands offering everything from pizza to sushi at Union Station (50 Massachusetts Ave. NE). One of the best eateries is **America** (see D.C. Ducks), with suitably American regional fare. **Johnny Rockets** (tel. 202/289–6969), a 1950s-style hamburger joint, also appeals to families.

THE CASTLE (SMITHSONIAN BUILDING)

In London castles may be for kings and queens, but here in Washington, the Castle is for us common folk who want to map out a day on the National Mall. And since it opens an hour before the other Mall museums, early risers can get a good jump on their adventures. Called the Castle because of its magnificent towers and turrets, this first Smithsonian building is a Norman-style structure made of red sandstone. Completed in 1855, it originally housed all of the Smithsonian's operations—hard to imagine now—including the science and art collections, research laboratories, and living quarters for the institution's first secretary and his family.

Start at the Castle's Smithsonian Information Center, where you can learn all about the museum, education, and research complex—16 museums and galleries (nine of which are on the Mall) and a zoo—that is Washington's Smithsonian Institution. A 20-minute video overview plays constantly. If your kids will sit still that long, you may get to watch it. Better yet, talk to the very knowledgeable volunteers, or pick up a brochure. Touch-screen

HEY, KIDS! In the 1890s American buffalo (a.k.a. bison) were kept in a pen behind the Castle. These once-numerous beasts had been hunted so relentlessly for decades that their numbers were dwindling. Determined to prevent their extinction, Samuel Pierpont Langley, the Smithsonian's third secretary, convinced Congress to provide a site where bison and other animals could be protected and displayed. It was the beginning of the National Zoo. Today, about 10,000 buffalo live on protected land, but no tracks remain here.

1000 Jefferson Dr. SW. Metro: Smithsonian

 Free

 Daily 9–5:30

 202/357–2020 recording, 202/357–2700
voice, 202/357–1729 TTY; www.si.edu

 2 and up

monitors at heights for both children and adults display information on the day's events. Interactive videos provide more detailed information on the museums as well as other attractions in the capital city. Push a button on the electronic map to locate Arlington National Cemetery or to light up the entire Metro system. A Braille map of the city wasn't designed for children, but draws them nonetheless.

The Castle doesn't have exhibits anymore, but some children are fascinated by the tomb of the institution's British benefactor, James Smithson, which is housed in the appropriately named Crypt Room. His bequest worth $508,318.46 in gold sovereigns established the Smithsonian.

On the other hand, if you're not an early riser and the day is hot, pause a while so you can cool off by strolling through the Enid A. Haupt Garden, behind the Castle, where one of the fountains spurts water onto the path.

KEEP IN MIND

You can't see the Smithsonian's entire collection of objects, artifacts, specimens, and creatures—more than 143 million and growing, due to gifts, purchases, and, at the zoo, births. At some museums, only 1%–2% of the collections are on display, but unlike the stuff under kids' beds, objects are cataloged and used in research.

EATS FOR KIDS More than 3 million people—15% of Smithsonian museum visitors—eat at the institution's cafeterias and restaurants. The following Mall museums have eateries (*see* each listing): the National Air and Space Museum, National Gallery of Art and Sculpture Garden, National Museum of American History, and National Museum of Natural History. Or grab a bagel and juice from **Seattle's Best Coffee** in the Smithsonian's Arts and Industries Building (900 Jefferson Dr., tel. 202/357–2627).

CHILDREN'S MUSEUM OF ROSE HILL MANOR PARK

The first place kids go in this historic home is the same one they seek out in most houses: the playroom. However, the playroom of this Georgian home, the last residence of the first elected governor of Maryland, is full of replicas of toys and games from more than 100 years ago: corncob checkers, a dollhouse, a rocking horse, a tea set, dress-up clothes, and mechanical coin banks. Lift a lever on these banks to move a penny from a whale to a boat, a monkey to a box, or Uncle Sam's arm to a little black bag.

Costumed guides meet families in the playroom, and the antique adventure continues. Upstairs there's a master bedroom, domestic quarters, a study room, and a child's bedroom with Early American toys. A 1½-hour tour at most historical sights would be too long for kids, but guides here are experienced in showing children what life was like during our country's infancy. Along the way, they explain how fireplaces, bed warmers, and windows were used in different weather. In addition, the tour includes numerous hands-on activities.

GETTING THERE Rose Hill Manor is well worth the 50-mile drive from D.C. Take I–270 north to U.S. 15 at Frederick, exiting at Motter Avenue. Turn left on 14th Street and left on North Market Street. The entrance is just past the Governor Thomas Johnson High School.

EATS FOR KIDS Pretzel and Pizza Creations (210 N. Market St., tel. 301/ 694–9299) puts a new twist on pretzels, whose 30 varieties include chocolate, peanut butter, and rainbow sprinkle. Children's books on shelves in the back and cups of cappuccino encourage kids and their parents to linger. At the **Village Restaurant** (4 E. Patrick St., tel. 301/662–1944), you can sit at stools in front of a 65-year-old marble counter and order milkshakes and sodas fresh from the fountain.

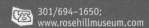

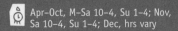

Back downstairs, children can card wool, operate a loom, add stitches to a quilt, or try out 19th-century cooking equipment. If the tour does get tiresome for your kids, however, you can escape to the gardens, where there's room to romp.

The tour itself continues outside to a one-room log cabin, a reminder that the majority of people in the early 1800s were not to the manner born. Most settlers lived in simple homesteads. In the blacksmith's shop, kids learn how 19th-century "smithies" spent most of their time repairing such ironwork as axes and chains. In the carriage museum, your children can find foot warmers in carriages and sleighs. Near the carriage museum, an Early American garden and orchard contains more than 100 species of herbs, flowers, fruits, and vegetables. If you're interested, the last tour stop is the requisite museum store, which carries postcards and inexpensive trinkets.

HEY, KIDS! While you're walking around Rose Hill Manor, think about the fact that houses hundreds of years ago had no closets, no bathrooms (not even running water), no electricity, no central heating, and no air-conditioning. See if you can find all the devices and solutions people employed instead of those modern conveniences.

CITY MUSEUM OF WASHINGTON, D.C.

Where have you been in Washington? Try to find your next D.C. destination on the map at the City Museum. While you can't fold this map up and put it in your pocket, you can crawl around on this 18-by-18-foot aerial map covered in glass. Identifying places is harder than it looks because no streets or sights are labeled.

A project of the Historical Society of Washington, D.C., the museum opened in 2003 to educate people about the families and folk who live here, not just the politicians and famous people we learn about in history books.

In "Washington Perspectives," the gallery with the map, exhibits in the corners are dedicated to four periods in Washington's history: pre–Civil War, post–Civil war, pre–World War II, and post–World War II. Pick up a wand and you can hear history in sound bites. Pull out dozens of drawers and you'll find mementos from each era. Listen as residents reveal what it was like to vote in a presidential election for the first time. (D.C. residents couldn't

HEY, KIDS! This museum is in the Carnegie Library building, which was first dedicated 100 years ago. This building is near and dear to many citizens of the District of Columbia because it was one of the first integrated public spaces in the city. (This means all people were welcome.) Although blacks couldn't shop in the same places or visit the museums that whites could, they could come to the Carnegie Library to learn. See if you can find the words "Science," "History," and "Poetry" on the building, as well as the names Plato, Homer, Galileo, Shakespeare, Newton, and Bacon. Hint: You'll need to look outside, too!

 801 K St. NW: Metro: Gallery Place/Chinatown

 202/383–1800; www.citymuseumdc.org

 $3 adults; $2 students of all ages (under 3 free); $7 adults or $5 students includes multimedia presentation

 Tu–Su 10–5 (open on Monday holidays)

 7 and up

vote for president until 1964 after Congress passed the 23rd amendment.) Open each of the four doors to reveal another era of history. Hear the oinks of pigs and clomping of horses' hoofs from a time when this area was a marketplace. Take a seat at the boarding house table and discover who really ran the place. And any kid who likes to create creatures from clay figurines will appreciate the sculptures by local artist Anna Johnson. These 9" models show people in settings from each era. But no visit is complete without seeing the multimedia show "Washington Stories." A tour guide, who looks three-dimensional, gets interrupted from giving her slide show as famous folks and even "go go" music rounds out the stories.

If your child digs D.C., check out the archaeology lab in the basement. Maybe you'll see the next museum artifact unearthed.

EATS FOR KIDS

If your child is hungry for more than knowledge in the museum, **Café Washington** offers sandwiches, soups, muffins, and more, provided by a local mother and her son. For a larger selection, cross K Street to the food court in the Technology Center (800 K St., no phone).

KEEP IN MIND Most families can see the multimedia show and exhibits in less than an hour. If any of the exhibits excite your child to learn more, the reference library is open to scholars of all ages. Librarians can help you research your own family's history, neighborhood history, and historic buildings. They can also help you figure out the date of old photographs.

CLAUDE MOORE COLONIAL
FARM AT TURKEY RUN

Back in the 1770s, children didn't have to go to school, wear shoes, or take a nightly bath. Some modern children might even think those early days were easy—that is, until they visit this re-created Colonial farm.

Here child volunteers portraying Colonial kids (when school is closed) explain that children couldn't go to school because they worked all day on the farm. Those who could fit into one of the few pairs of shoes a family might own were lucky, as they were less likely to suffer from sore feet. Frequent baths weren't considered healthful—nor were they practical, since heating enough water for a tub took a long time.

Even when the Colonial kids aren't here, you and your children can watch a pair of historical interpreters, dressed in period clothing, demonstrate how a farming couple eked out a living by tending to tobacco and wheat fields, a vegetable garden, farm animals, and family chores.

KEEP IN MIND One word of warning: Encourage your kids to go to the bathroom before you arrive. The farm is equipped with the modern-day equivalent of outhouses (the portable toilet).

HEY, KIDS! When Colonial kids played, they either used their imaginations or made toys out of things that had no monetary value and weren't needed elsewhere. They made marbles out of clay and turned split sapling trees into hoops, which they rolled on the ground with a stick. Try rolling a hula hoop with a stick. It's harder than you might think, and you don't need batteries.

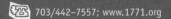 6310 Georgetown Pike, McLean, VA

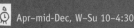 $3 ages 13 and up, $2 children 3–12; Market Fair $5 ages 13 and up, $2.50 children 3–12

 Apr–mid-Dec, W–Su 10–4:30

703/442–7557; www.1771.org

2 and up

A dirt path winds around an orchard, fields, a tobacco barn, a pond, a hog pen, and an English-style, one-room farmhouse. The walk is comfortable, and a well-napped preschooler can make the trip without wearing out. Pushing a stroller along the root-laden path is tricky, but it is possible.

During Market Fairs, held the third full weekends in May, July, and October, families enjoy making Colonial crafts (about $1 each), listening to music, and watching puppet shows. And just as in the 1770s, you can eat and shop. Check out the rosemary chicken and vegetables roasted over a fire, hot pies, and more. Reproductions of 18th-century pottery, jewelry, fragrant soaps, clothing, and toys are for sale on Market Fair days, too.

By the end of the day, your kids will probably have discovered that Colonial life was indeed tough, but you'll have discovered that a trip to Claude Moore is easy.

EATS FOR KIDS If you packed a lunch, grab one of the picnic tables at the farm entrance. A few miles away, the **McLean Family Restaurant** (1321 Chain Bridge Rd., tel. 703/356–9883) has been serving Greek and American dishes for more than 30 years. At **Rocco's Italian Restaurant** (1357 Chain Bridge Rd., tel. 703/821–3736), child-size pizzas are best-sellers, but those with more sophisticated palates can order manicotti, rigatoni, and ravioli. After eating, kids (and adults) can get a lollipop for the road.

COLLEGE PARK AVIATION MUSEUM

Walk by the animatronic Wilbur Wright and he'll tell you about teaching pilots to fly in 1909. But children don't have to take Wilbur's word for it that learning to fly was thrilling. They'll see it for themselves at this interactive museum dedicated to early aviation.

Your children will be challenged and exhilarated as they turn and pull levers, knobs, and switches on flight simulators. They can try starting a plane's engine, not by turning a key as it's done today, but the way it was done before World War I, by turning a propeller. (Hint: Make sure no one is in the way and push down as hard as you can. Then step back. It's loud!) Your kids can even dress like pilots of yore, donning goggles, silk scarves, and helmets to pose for pictures against an airplane backdrop. (Be sure to bring a camera.) Turn on the fan to set the scarf blowing in the wind.

Also inside, a full-scale replica of the 1911 Wright B Aeroplane, a restored 1918 Curtiss Jenny, a 1932-era Monocoupe, and a Berliner Helicopter grace the largest gallery of this

EATS FOR KIDS If your kids just want to watch planes, bring lunch and eat on the museum balcony, overlooking the airport. Or follow the planes painted on a path outside to the aviation-theme **94th Air Squadron restaurant** (5240 Paint Branch Pkwy., tel. 301/699–9400), where big-band music plays. Here you can watch the airport action, but the food is as inconsistent as airplane meals. To take off for guaranteed good eats, try the original **Ledo's** (2420 University Blvd., tel. 301/422–8622), about 2 miles away. Some people insist that Ledo's pizza—with cheese so gooey you need a knife and fork—is Maryland's most delicious.

1985 Cpl. Frank Scott Dr., College Park, MD.
Metro: College Park

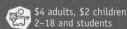
$4 adults, $2 children
2–18 and students

Daily 10–5

301/864–6029;
www.collegeparkaviationmuseum.com

2 and up

airy museum, which opened in 1998. If you notice a similarity to the National Air and Space Museum (*see* #34), you're not imagining it; both museums were designed by the same architectural firm. But here you can see and do everything in an hour and you won't have to worry about losing your children in crowds.

Outside there's still more to see and do. Children ages 5 and under get a feel for flying by riding around in wooden planes on a mini-runway. Gaze out the museum's large glass wall onto College Park Airport, the world's oldest continually operating airport. Referred to as the "cradle of aviation," it lays claim to the first Army aviation school, first U.S. Postal Service flight, and first female passenger to fly in the United States. But those facts probably won't interest your youngster as much as simply watching the small, single-engine planes take off and land.

GETTING THERE

The nearest Metro stop, College Park, is a significant walk from the museum (about 15 minutes), and since it's on the Green Line, it means a transfer for many people. Driving is probably an easier way to get here, and parking is plentiful.

KEEP IN MIND For a list of what's happening on the day you visit, check the flight desk at the front of the museum. It may list How Things Fly, of interest to older kids, or Peter Pan Club activities, such as making paper airplanes, for preschoolers. In addition, when Maryland or Prince George's County public schools are closed, the museum sponsors aviation craft activities. If you don't make your own souvenir, though, you may want to take home a flight of fancy from the museum's gift shop, which is full of aviation toys and games, many under $5.

CORCORAN GALLERY OF ART

57

Create a flip book like the flip art in this book. Make a mosaic. Turn everyday objects into works of art. These are some of the activities in store as part of monthly Sunday Traditions, when one of the oldest U.S. museums offers kids workshops and tours. In addition, a few times each year the Corcoran holds Family Days, and the whole museum transforms into a family free-for-all. To celebrate those famous birthdays, for example, a February program may involve looking for portraits of presidents. Each of the Family Days and Sunday Traditions is different. Call for a calendar.

If you can't make one of these events, you can still create a fun family adventure by sharing your enthusiasm for art with your children. The permanent collection at the Corcoran, one of the few large, private museums in Washington outside the Smithsonian family, numbers more than 14,000 works, including paintings by the first great American portraitists: John Singleton Copley, Gilbert Stuart, and Rembrandt Peale. In fact, the portrait on the $1 bill was modeled on Stuart's *Portrait of George Washington*. A replica (by the artist's

KEEP IN MIND Sunday Traditions are a tradition for many local families. Registration is required. You can—and many parents do—sign up five weeks in advance. In fact, it's best to call at least four weeks ahead of time or risk having the program you want be full.

HEY, KIDS! Check out the huge painting *George Washington Before Yorktown*, by Rembrandt Peale. One of 17 children, five of whom were named for artists, Peale took some liberties with reality. Washington's horse, Nelson, was actually brown, but Peale painted him white, perhaps to stand out against the mainly brown background. (Incidentally, at times Washington did own white horses.) After the Revolution, Nelson was retired to Mount Vernon and, in recognition of his service, was never again ridden or required to work.

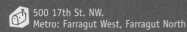
500 17th St. NW.
Metro: Farragut West, Farragut North

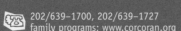
202/639–1700, 202/639–1727
family programs; www.corcoran.org

$5 adults, $3 students
13–18; $8 families of any
size; free on Thursdays
after 5

M, W, and F–Su 10–5, Th 10–9;
tours M, W, and F 12, Th 7:30,
Sa and Su 12 and 2:30

5 and up

own hand, not a copy by someone else) is at the gallery. Ask at the front desk if it's hanging that day; if it is, hand your kids dollar bills and have them try to find it. Photography and works by contemporary American artists are also strengths here.

If your children appreciate beauty, see the 13th-century stained-glass window that originally hung in France's Soissons Cathedral. When the sun shines, watch the colors seemingly melt onto the floor. If your kids like cartoons, check out the collection by French caricaturist Honoré Daumier. The exaggerated facial features in his caricatures of politicians eventually got him in trouble. (Worse than being grounded—he went to jail.) If your kids love action, show them the buffalo hunt in *Last of the Buffalo,* by Albert Bierstadt. See if they can find a coyote, a prairie dog, an elk, and antelopes. It's the thrill of the hunt, after all, that makes a museum experience even more memorable.

EATS FOR KIDS The Corcoran Gallery's **Café des Artistes** looks too elegant for little children, but high chairs let you know that even the littlest child is welcome. The Corcoran's Jazz Gospel Brunch on Sunday is festive for families. If you'd rather dine on paper plates than china, **Burrito Brothers** (1825 I St. NW, tel. 202/887–8266), a Mexican fast-food restaurant, is a few blocks away in the Ronald Reagan Building. For other casual eateries, *see* the DAR Museum and the White House.

CRAYOLA WORKS

At this combination store and studio in Arundel Mills, MD, kids move beyond drawing with sticks of colored wax on paper to creating their own masterpieces. In the store, kids color with Crayola's 50 most popular crayons arranged in bins around a lazy Susan that encircle a tower of crayons that stretches to the ceiling. Kids can also watch their faces morph like Silly Putty on a computer screen. And at least every hour, the store offers "make it and take it" projects. Intermingled among the displays is tons of stuff to buy, including multicolor crayons matching all shades of skin, backpacks, and even projects tested in the studio.

For the most exciting adventure at Crayola Works, follow the winding rainbow on the floor to the Creativity Studio, the only one like it in the country. Here, kids choose from a whole menu of creations packaged in bright cardboard boxes with handles. Everything your child needs to create a masterpiece rolls down in a carton from a chute near the ceiling. Crayola takes the guesswork out of which product works best on which surface by putting everything

KEEP IN MIND Dress your kids in clothes that can withstand another stain. Some of the paints are permanent. Also, kids are not only *allowed* to color in places that would be taboo at home, they're *encouraged!* They draw and write on walls, windows and even a Volkswagon Bug. All activities require your attendance unless your child is enrolled in a class or attending a birthday party. Then you can take advantage of shopping. But you may have more fun creating your own project!

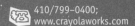 7000 Arundel Mills Circle, Hanover, MD
(Ann Arundel Mills Mall)

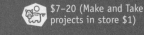 $7–20 (Make and Take
projects in store $1)

 M–Sa 10–9:30, Su 11–7
(extended holiday hours)

410/799-0400;
www.crayolaworks.com

2–12

together. Activities change according to seasons and holidays. Some of the projects have included decorating wind chimes, bird houses, mirrors, keepsake boxes, and even soccer balls—a favorite among preteens.

If your children need to find just the right stencil, sparkly paint, or inspiration, a member of the "Color Crew" can come to their rescue. Many of the staff study art or elementary education. Perhaps more important, they're also people who know how to be silly—but they also know how to give genuine feedback.

Kids who finish their projects early can wrap their own crayons with paper, draw on computer screens, and make short films with clay figures. Kiddies too young to participate in projects can look in a fun house mirror and crawl around beanbag chairs in the play area.

GETTING THERE
Crayola Works is worth the drive from Washington. Take I-95 north to exit 43A (Route 100 East) to exit 10A, Arundel Mills Boulevard. From 295 North, proceed to Arundel Mills Boulevard. Crayola Works is in Arundel Mills Mall between Outdoor World and Jillians.

EATS FOR KIDS At the **Crayola Café,** kids can pick up a snack, such as juice boxes, cookies, and crackers; parents might prefer a cup of coffee or tea. Each item is $1. For more than a munchie, the mall's Food Court sells lemonade and hot dogs, tacos, and sandwiches in a space as colorful as Crayola Works.

DAR MUSEUM

At this museum, modern kids discover what life was like 150 years or so B.C. (before computers) as part of the Colonial Adventure program (reservations required). The journey begins with dressing the part. Boys wear decorative collars, silk vests, workmen's aprons, and three-corner caps. Girls don calico bonnets and long skirts with white aprons, because proper Colonial ladies never showed their hair or their ankles. Docents, who are all DAR (Daughters of the American Revolution) members and who also wear Colonial garb, then lead the children on a special tour, explaining the exhibits and describing life in Colonial America. Along the way children visit the Touch of Independence exhibit, where they play with Early American toys, such as a cradle and Noah's ark, and enjoy a pretend tea party. Docents demonstrate facets of Colonial life, including candle making. A Braille flag of the United States is also a big hit.

While the younger ones are visiting their own version of 18th-century America, parents and older siblings—or anyone else who isn't the right age, here at the right time, or

KEEP IN MIND If your children have particular interests, inform your docent. Kids with an ear for music should see the antique instruments in the Rhode Island room. You may be surprised to learn that early Americans were more likely to listen to Yankee Doodle–type tunes than Bach.

HEY, KIDS! Move over Paul Revere or, better yet, dismount! At 16, Sybil Ludington rode off on her horse to warn folks that the British had come to Danbury, Connecticut. Sybil's ride on April 25, 1777, was longer and riskier than Revere's ride two years earlier. Sybil rode sidesaddle on a big bay horse for 40 miles—26 miles more than Revere—through a dangerous no-man's land between British and American lines. A statue and painting of Sybil are in the museum.

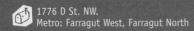

1776 D St. NW.
Metro: Farragut West, Farragut North

 Free

M–F 9:30–4, Sa 9–5; tours M–F 10–2:30,
Sa 8:30–5; Colonial Adventure usually
Sept–May, 1st and 3rd Sa of mth 1:30 and 3

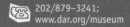 202/879-3241;
www.dar.org/museum

 5 and up, Colonial
Adventure 5–7

in the right mood for the Colonial Adventure—can take their own docent-led tour, held for small groups during the day. These tours tend to interest girls especially, as docents weave tales of women's contributions into their descriptions of many of the museum's 32 period rooms, named after states.

Your kids might think the Oklahoma room, set up like a Colonial kitchen, is cool. (Try to find the toaster.) The Georgia room depicts a Savannah tavern, where citizens gathered for the state's first reading of the Declaration of Independence. In the New Hampshire room, docents describe 18th- and 19th-century dolls. And the Wisconsin room depicts a one-room house like those that only quite fortunate families could afford in Colonial times. Your children might just leave the DAR Museum not only with an understanding of Colonial life but also with an appreciation of contemporary life.

EATS FOR KIDS The lines are short, but the list of selections is long at the **Bread Line** (1751 Pennsylvania Ave. NW, tel. 202/822–8900), where you can get fresh smoothies, sandwiches, and salads weekdays. **Georgia Brown's** (950 15th St. NW, tel. 202/393–4499) offers down-home, yet upscale Southern-style cooking on tables covered with white butcher paper, perfect for crayon creations.

D.C. DUCKS

What do you get when you cross a tour bus with a boat? A duck, of course—that is, a D.C. Duck. Your family can tour the city by both land and water without leaving your seats aboard these unusual amphibious vehicles: standard 2½-ton GM trucks in water-tight shells with propellers that seat 28 intrepid passengers.

During the 1½-hour ride, a wise-quacking captain entertains with anecdotes and historical trivia about Washington's memorials, monuments, and historic buildings. The captain may even quiz kids about sights along the way. Answer correctly and ding—the bell rings! For example, the captain may ask what boats are represented by the three flags near the statue of Christopher Columbus in front of Union Station. No, the answer isn't the *Love Boat,* the S.S. *Minnow,* and the *Titanic,* but rather the *Nina,* the *Pinta,* and the *Santa María.* But the part of the tour that quacks kids up the most is quacking themselves—both at tourists in town and real ducks on the water.

EATS FOR KIDS Duck into Union Station (*see* Capital Children's Museum), a bustling train station where inaugural balls have been held. More than 35 vendors offer fast food from around the world. If you prefer a restaurant, try **America** (tel. 202/682–9555), whose menu of regional foods lives up to the expansive name. Kid-pleasing offerings include peanut butter with marshmallow cream sandwiches. In November and December, request gallery seating for a bird's-eye view of the station's train exhibit.

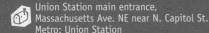
Union Station main entrance,
Massachusetts Ave. NE near N. Capitol St.
Metro: Union Station

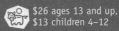
$26 ages 13 and up,
$13 children 4–12

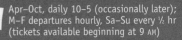
Apr–Oct, daily 10–5 (occasionally later);
M–F departures hourly, Sa–Su every ½ hr
(tickets available beginning at 9 AM)

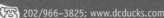
202/966–3825; www.dcducks.com

4 and up

Starting along the city streets, the Duck keeps pace with traffic. Eventually it moves into the river, where it motors along at a pace only slightly faster than the feathered version for which it was named. Here kids cover their ears while watching planes take off from Ronald Reagan National Airport. As jets fly overhead, you may hear a popping sound. Little air cannons on the runways alert ducks and other birds to stay away, so they aren't killed by the engines.

While on the Potomac, your children can glimpse the Pentagon, headquarters of the Department of Defense; the Anacostia Helicopter Station, home of the presidential helicopters; and the War College, formerly Fort McNair, where the conspirators who plotted to kill Lincoln were tried, convicted, and hanged. Often children are invited to take the captain's seat and steer the Duck. When you're all done, you can add waddling through Washington and cruising around the Potomac on a Duck to your list of D.C. experiences.

HEY, KIDS! Ducks, known as DUKWs in World War II, were created to transport soldiers and supplies from ships to areas without ports. More than 21,000 DUKWs were produced, mostly by women. After the war, the Army left many DUKWs abroad, and they can still be found around the world.

KEEP IN MIND If your family is more into bikes than boats or if you'd just like to tour the city a different way, consider a **Bike the Sites Tour** (1100 Pennsylvania Ave., tel. 202/842–2453; www.bikethesites.com). For $40 per adult, $30 for kids 12 and under (including use of a bike), you can take a 3-hour tour covering approximately 8 miles and 55 sights. Along the way, a guide discusses history, lore, and even scandals of the capital city. The trip is appropriate for ages 9 and older, and reservations are recommended.

DISCOVERY CREEK CHILDREN'S MUSEUM

Would your children like to play dirt detectives? Romp in a swamp? Build a volcano? Watch a chameleon change colors? Discovery Creek's innovative nature programs combine outdoor adventures, art projects or experiments, and live animal demonstrations. Weekdays are primarily devoted to school groups during the school year and a camp during the summer, but on weekends the museum hosts drop-in (not drop-off) programs for families.

In historic Glen Echo Park (*see* #47), Discovery Creek was once home to horses. Although the horses are long gone, the museum still brings the outdoors—and its creatures— in. Museum programs reflect themes that change at least twice a year. When the theme was "wetlands," three feet of mud was dumped on the floor, tall grass grew, and tadpoles made homes in indoor ponds. If the theme is "the desert," you'll find three feet of sand instead. A paddock that once contained horses has been transformed into a children's botanical garden. Here kids play in a heron's nest tree fort, a wetlands area with ponds, bamboo trails, and an underground tunnel where they can see root

HEY, KIDS!

Did you know that chocolate, chewing gum, and bananas come from rain-forest plants? Did you know that most insects can pick out four tastes (bitter, salty, sweet, and sour), just as you can? You can do experiments and crafts here to make these facts come alive.

EATS FOR KIDS Though you can't fish in the Minnehaha Creek, you can get fish from the **Pepperidge Farm Thrift Store** (7309 MacArthur Blvd., Bethesda, tel. 301/ 229-0953)—goldfish crackers to be exact. The expiration date may be past, but you'll pay about half the retail price for crackers and cookies. Two doors down from what kids call the "fishy cracker store" are a **7-Eleven** (7305 MacArthur Blvd., tel. 301/229- 4474) and **Glen Echo Pizza & Subs** (7307 MacArthur Blvd., tel. 301/263-0414), where you can carry out slices of pizza or thick french fries covered with ketchup, cheese, or barbecue sauce served in sturdy paper cups.

7300 MacArthur Blvd., Glen Echo, MD

 $5

 Sa 10–3, Su 11–3

202/337–5111;
www.discoverycreek.org

2–11

systems of plants. In a stable where horses once slept, your children can scale new heights on a climbing wall.

One of the smallest museums in the area, Discovery Creek provides an intimate place to learn. The scope of exploration isn't restricted, however, as every program takes advantage of a nature trail in the woods behind the museum. Hundreds of insects scurry around a fallen tree trunk, teaching about soil decomposition and animal habitats. A steep trail leads to Minnehaha Creek, where kids traverse stepping stones, searching for crayfish and other water-lovers.

The museum cares for a menagerie of animals, some of which were rescued and raised by friends of the museum. Along with the wildlife and plants in the forest, these critters provide exciting, tangible activities that help kids learn about nature.

KEEP IN MIND To ensure that your family has a good time, remember these safety and comfort tips. Make sure everyone dresses for adventure; good walking shoes are essential. If your children are young, you may need to provide a hand when climbing down the steep trail and over the creek's stepping stones. Be prepared for the unexpected. A child who is fascinated one minute could be frightened the next as a bird expands its wings or a snake uncurls. And if your family enjoys its visit here, stay and enjoy Glen Echo's other attractions.

DISCOVERY THEATER

In the midst of the mammoth museums on the Mall is a small theater that brings both our national heritage and other cultures to life. Here kids can delight in the antics of Robert Strong as he juggles bowling balls, bananas, and even rakes. He even teaches a few tricks of the trade. On a more serious note, history opens up as kids watch *Black Diamond* and learn about Satchel Paige, philosopher and Negro League baseball player. From popular tales to well-told, lesser-known tales from around the world, the Smithsonian's Discovery Theater lives up to its name as a place for discovery.

In the West Wing of the Arts and Industries Building, Discovery Theater is the scene of plays, puppet shows, and storytelling. Puppeteers can usually be seen manipulating their puppets in the background. Young audiences are often encouraged to take part, too, by singing, clapping, or helping to develop characters and plots. And since you're never more than 10 rows away from the action at Discovery Theater, which seats up to 200 people, close encounters between the audience and actors are easy.

KEEP IN MIND The "Weekend" section of the *Washington Post* lists Discovery Theater performances as well as other kid-oriented shows around town. Whichever show you select (and reservations are recommended), plan to arrive 15 minutes early. If you're attending a 10 o'clock show, go around to the west entrance in the Enid A. Haupt garden, where the doors open early for Discovery Theater patrons only. Otherwise, the building itself doesn't open until 10.

Arts and Industries Building,
900 Jefferson Dr. SW.
Metro: Smithsonian

 $5 ages 3 and up

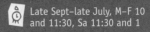 Late Sept–late July, M–F 10
and 11:30, Sa 11:30 and 1

202/357-1500;
www.DiscoveryTheater.org

 2½–14

Though most performances are geared to preschoolers through second graders, some are for older children and teens. Many of these performances are held in the 550-seat Baird Auditorium at the Museum of Natural History. Performances for older kids tend to be factually based presentations about historical figures or events. Past examples have included *Sister Rain, Brother Sun,* a puppet show; *Angel in the Battlefield,* a play about Clara Barton; and *Come Sign with Me,* by a performer who is deaf. Often productions are tied in with local schools' curricula.

Throughout the year, Discovery Theater celebrates special themes. For example, in late September and October, Hispanic Heritage takes center stage, and in November, tales from Native Americans are highlighted. The most popular month for performances is February, when Black History Month is celebrated with songs, stories, and plays about cowboys, heroes, and more.

HEY, KIDS! Ride a painted pony—with stripes, polka dots, even clown faces on their saddles—on a carousel in front of the building. But it's the lone dragon that attracts the most attention. Sometimes kids let others ahead of them so they're first in line for the next cycle.

EATS FOR KIDS For a hot pretzel or an ice cream, check out the street vendors in front of the building. For a complete meal, walk over to the National Air and Space Museum's restaurants. Across the Mall, both the National Museum of Natural History and the National Museum of American History have restaurants (*see* listings for each).

EAST POTOMAC PARK

Bring your camera (everyone else does) to take a picture of your children giving high-fives to a hand more than 100 times larger than their own, sliding down a huge leg, or sitting in a monstrous mouth and living to tell about it. Or better yet, join in, and climb all over *The Awakening*, an immense statue of a man who is half buried in the ground. For some kids, he looks like a monster. Others think the bearded gent looks like dad when he's waking up. Either way, he's incredibly cool, sitting (or rather lying) at the tip of this Hains Point park, a 328-acre tongue of land that hangs down from the Tidal Basin between the Washington Channel to the east and the Potomac River to the west.

More traditional forms of recreation—tennis, golf, swimming, and miniature golf—are also available at the park and for prices that tend to be lower than at comparable enterprises.

GETTING THERE The best route is Ohio Drive, heading south, or Maine Avenue SW, turning off near the 14th Street bridge, heading west. Follow signs carefully. Ohio Drive is closed to traffic 3 PM–6 AM on summer weekends and holidays. Going by Metro is not an option—at least not with kids. The nearest stop is a mile away.

EATS FOR KIDS Pack a picnic or visit the **golf course snack bar** (tel. 202/554–7660) for a jumbo burger or sandwich. For seafood, pick a restaurant along Maine Avenue or visit its seafood market (*see* Franklin Delano Roosevelt Memorial for both). At **Captain White's Seafood City** (1100 Maine Ave. SW, tel. 202/484–2722), East Coast fish are displayed in rows. Look carefully: the stand is actually in water. The captain and his neighbors don't have seating, but you can carry out crab soup, shrimp, fish sandwiches, and more.

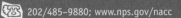 1100 Ohio Dr. SW, at Maine Ave.

 Free; some attractions charge

Daily sunrise–sunset; pool Memorial Day wknd–Labor Day

202/485–9880; www.nps.gov/nacc

2 and up

Built during the midget golf craze of the 1920s, East Potomac Mini Golf is the oldest miniature golf course in the area. Unlike newer courses, it doesn't sport any caves, windmills, or fountains, but it does have native stonework and ponds with goldfish, water lilies, and a bridge. Golfers who love to do more than putter around will appreciate the challenging greens; each hole is a par-3. Kids who have moved beyond the miniature may play on two regular 9-hole golf courses or an additional 18-hole course, or just practice on the double-tier driving range or putting greens.

The long road and the parking lot make a picturesque (and perfectly flat) place to teach your child to ride a bike. The park also has outdoor tennis courts as well as courts under a bubble, which make tennis playable year-round. Reservations should be made early. A swimming pool—alas with neither diving board nor baby pool—and fishing along the Potomac (tel. 202/727–4582 for permits) round out the sporting opportunities.

HEY, KIDS! Most of J. Seward Johnson Jr.'s sculptures depict life-size people doing everyday things, like playing chess or reading the newspaper. At 70 feet, *The Awakening* is Johnson's largest work and hardly life-size. Do you think the giant is doing an everyday thing?

FORD'S THEATRE NATIONAL HISTORIC SITE

The events of April 14, 1865, which shocked the nation and closed this theater, continue to fascinate both young and old. On that night, during a performance of *Our American Cousin,* John Wilkes Booth entered the state box on the balcony and assassinated Abraham Lincoln. The stricken president was carried across the street to the house of tailor William Peterson, where he died the next morning.

Allow about an hour to take a self-guided tour of Ford's Theatre and the Lincoln Museum (in the lower level) and to cross the street to Peterson House to see the bedroom where Lincoln died. (Allow more time during busy spring and summer months, since you may have to wait in line for a tour.) A Junior Ranger handout, aimed at kids 6–12, sends young history detectives on a hunt to find the box where Lincoln was shot, the Derringer pistol that Booth used, and the suit that Lincoln wore that night. The book also includes activities ranging from a connect-the-dots picture of Lincoln's top hat to word scrambles. After completing the activities, each child receives a Junior Ranger badge.

HEY, KIDS! How tall are you? Probably not as tall as Abraham Lincoln, who was 6'4"—even more extraordinary in his day, because poor diet often stunted children's growth. To see where you'd come up to on the former president, stand next to his full-size picture. Hint: You and Honest Abe side by side would make a cool photograph.

Ford's Theatre: 511 10th St. NW;
Peterson House: 516 10th St. NW.
Metro: Metro Center

202/426-6924;
www.nps.gov/foth

 Free

 Daily 9–5; tours fifteen minutes after the hour
9:15–4:15; theater closed during rehearsals and
matinees (usually Th and Sa–Su); call ahead.

7 and up

Throughout the day when the theater is open, National Park Service rangers and volunteers give 15-minute talks (some quite theatrical) about Lincoln's assassination. If you miss a presentation and your children have questions, encourage them to read the signs that accompany the displays in the museum (open even when the theater is not). Large type makes them more readable than typical museum signage. If you still have questions, talk to a ranger. It might seem strange at first to see rangers in museum settings instead of big national parks, but since Washington, D.C., is a federal district full of national monuments and historic sites, rangers are a common sight and a great resource.

KEEP IN MIND
Every year from Thanksgiving through New Year's, the ghosts of Christmases past, present, and future come to the Ford's Theatre stage in Charles Dickens's classic tale *A Christmas Carol*. (The rest of the year, performances tend to be serious adult plays.) Call 202/347–4833 for information.

EATS FOR KIDS Older kids love the **Hard Rock Cafe** (999 E St. NW, tel. 202/737–7625), which mixes rock memorabilia and tunes. For live tunes at lunchtime and lots of hot sandwiches, check out **Potbelly** (555 12th St., tel. 202/347–7100). The "wreck" is loaded with a variety of meat. The "Big Jack," named for the owner's son, is a classic PB&J. For kids who haven't graduated from Raffi to rock and roll or if there's a long wait, the food court at the **Old Post Office Pavilion** (1100 Pennsylvania Ave. NW, tel. 202/289–4224) may be better.

FRANKLIN DELANO ROOSEVELT MEMORIAL

If you visit this memorial to our 32nd president with older children, take your time walking through its four outdoor "rooms" or galleries—each symbolic of one of Roosevelt's four terms. Waterfalls and reflecting pools are interspersed throughout, good for dangling toes. Pause in the granite passageways between the galleries, engraved with some of Roosevelt's most famous quotes, including "The only thing we have to fear is fear itself." If you come with toddlers, however, head straight to the third room. Here, though youngsters can't sit on Roosevelt's lap, they can pet Fala, Roosevelt's Scottish terrier. The tips of Fala's ears shine from all the attention.

Assuming you come here for more than Fala, there's plenty to absorb. Challenge your children to look closely at the big bronze wall of faces in the second room; it depicts people put back to work after the Depression. See if you can find two men planting trees, an artist stirring paint, one farmer gathering oranges, and another driving a tractor. There's even a girl painting and a boy sculpting. Also in the second gallery, handprints along the

HEY, KIDS!

Fala was famous in his day. He sat at the feet of his master and British Prime Minister Winston Churchill when they signed the Atlantic Charter in 1941. For merchandise featuring the presidential pooch, check out the gift shop. A portion of the proceeds benefits the National Park Service.

EATS FOR KIDS For refreshments, see the listing for the Lincoln Memorial. A short drive away, **Maine Avenue Seafood Market** (1100 Maine Ave. SW) carries fresh fish and shellfish. Maine Avenue also contains seven waterside restaurants, including local seafood powerhouse **Phillips Flagship** (900 Water St. SW, tel. 202/488–8515). All have terraces overlooking the Washington Channel and the boats moored there.

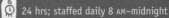

columns, representing the working hands of the American people, encourage you to touch. With help from parents, even babies can put their hands on prints. In the fourth room, a statue honors first lady Eleanor Roosevelt, a shy child who became a vocal spokesperson for human rights.

More than recognizing FDR's contributions, the memorial teaches children about history, war, and even disability. Due to polio, Roosevelt used a wheelchair for the last 24 years of his life, and a statue of him in the little wheelchair he made for himself was added to the memorial in 2001, after years of controversy.

Though the FDR Memorial is a good place for children, it's even better for grandparents, many of whom lived through the Depression and World War II. And perhaps it's at its best when shared by three (or four) generations.

KEEP IN MIND In the early 20th century, FDR contracted polio, at age 39, which left him paralyzed from the waist down. But when the memorial debuted, there wasn't much evidence of Roosevelt's disability, as there wasn't while he was president. He used a wheelchair, but kept his disability hidden from public view, except when visiting American war-wounded. Try asking older kids what's more important—that Roosevelt be seen realistically and as a role model for the disabled or that his desire not to have people see his disability be honored.

FREDERICK DOUGLASS NATIONAL
HISTORIC SITE

M ost tours of historic mansions dwell on how the wealthy lived—their fancy four-poster beds, oil paintings, mahogany furniture, and beautiful china. Your children can see these things at Cedar Hill, Frederick Douglass's last home, but the main focus is on this remarkable man, who paved a path to freedom and equality for all people.

One-hour tours (reservations recommended for groups of more than 5) begin on the hour (except noon) in the visitor center, where a wall is devoted to this prolific speaker and writer's quotations. Among the more famous ones is, "I would unite with anybody to do right and with nobody to do wrong." Here your children can shake hands with the bronze statue of Douglass, shiny gold from all that touching. The visitor center also has family photographs and a gift shop with books about Douglass.

Next you can watch the 17-minute film *Fighter for Freedom: The Frederick Douglass Story*. Douglass knew neither his mother, a slave, nor the identity of his father, a white man. At age 8, he

KEEP IN MIND To enhance your children's appreciation of Cedar Hill, talk about Frederick Douglass, the Civil War, and the Civil Rights movement before you arrive. Though *Fighter for Freedom: The Frederick Douglass Story* is enlightening, this short film depicts a graphic beating he got when he was a slave. Some children and even adults find it disturbing, not just because of the violence but because it confronts a shameful part of our history. Encourage your kids to talk about their feelings and ask questions of you and the rangers.

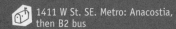 1411 W St. SE. Metro: Anacostia, then B2 bus

 202/426–5961 or 202/619–7222, 800/967–2283 reservations; www.nps.gov/frdo

 Free, $2 per person for reservations (groups of 5 or more)

 Mid-Apr–mid-Oct, daily 9–5 (last tour 4); mid-Oct–mid-Apr, daily 9–4 (last tour 3)

9 and up

was sold to a man in Baltimore, where he was exposed to the "mystery of reading" and decided that education was "the pathway to freedom." At 20 he escaped and became an abolitionist, women's rights activist, author, editor of an antislavery newspaper, minister to Haiti, and the most respected 19th-century African-American orator.

After the film, follow a park ranger to Cedar Hill, the first designated African American National Historic Site. Rangers focus on Douglass's life when in the house, first with Anna Murray, his wife of 40 years, and after her death, with second wife, Helen Pitts, who was not only 20 years his junior but also white. He simply explained that his first wife was the color of his mother, his second the color of his father. Though the tour is best for children who have studied American history, rangers are skilled at engaging kids as young as kindergartners. Children learn not only about the past but also about the importance of freedom and equality, even today.

EATS FOR KIDS
Unfortunately, the only place you're allowed to eat here is on the grassy hill near the visitor center, next to the parking lot, but there are no picnic tables. So you might want to eat before or after your visit. Also see East Potomac Park.

HEY, KIDS! Check out the portraits here. Many of the people represented were abolitionists (people who worked to end slavery), suffragists (people who sought to give women the right to vote), or, like Douglass, both. Look for Susan B. Anthony, John Brown, Elizabeth Cady Stanton, and Harriet Tubman. You can also search for a checkerboard, music box, invalid chair, peacock feathers, and dumbbells. What you won't find are Douglass's books—more than 1,200 of them—because they're stored in a temperature-controlled environment to last for future generations to study.

GLEN ECHO PARK

Years ago, Washingtonians took the trolley to Glen Echo's amusement park. Though neither the amusement park nor the trolley survives (and the closest Metro isn't close), Glen Echo, on the D.C. border, is still a magnificent and easily accessible park. It offers kids almost as many choices of activities as the historic Dentzel Carousel, in the park's center, offers choices of mounts, which range from a painted pony and a majestic lion to a saber-toothed tiger and an ostrich.

The arts thrive here. The 192-seat Adventure Theater stages such children's productions as *Charlotte's Web, Robin Hood,* and *Bunnicula* weekends year-round. Children sprawl on carpeted steps along with their families. At the Puppet Co. Playhouse, skilled puppeteers manipulate a variety of puppets in classic plays and stories. *Nutcracker,* in winter, is one of the most popular productions. After performances, puppeteers often greet children. Reservations are recommended for this popular puppet place.

KEEP IN MIND
Glen Echo was founded by two brothers, Edwin and Edward Baltzley, inventors of the egg beater. The brothers fell under the spell of the short-lived Chautauqua movement, an organization that promoted education to the masses. Glen Echo is still a place of learning, and has held classes on mosaics and rock guitar.

HEY, KIDS!
Recycling is hardly a new concept. Just step into the Clara Barton House for a taste of how people recycled a century ago. Newspapers weren't put out in bins to be collected in front of your house; they were put into the house as insulation. Old sheets weren't cut up for Halloween costumes; they were ripped to make bandages for the war wounded. And 19th-century recyclers didn't have to worry about plastic soda bottles; they hadn't been invented yet.

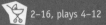
Nature holds its own at Glen Echo Park. In the former stables, a second Discovery Creek Children's Museum (*see* #53) offers nature programs with live animal demonstrations, crafts, and outdoor adventures. A local Eagle Scout candidate established nature trails around Minnehaha Creek, near the museum.

History has its place, too, and children who have studied the Civil War or women's history may enjoy a tour of the Clara Barton National Historic Site, near the park entrance. Known as the "angel of the battlefield" for nursing wounded soldiers, Clara Barton founded the American Red Cross. Rangers conduct hourly tours that give insight into her life and Glen Echo at the turn of the last century.

Last, but certainly not least, the park is also a great spot for recreation. When your kids need to let off steam, there's plenty of space to run around and a playground with a teeter-totter that can accommodate a dozen children.

EATS FOR KIDS When the carousel at Glen Echo is open (May–September, Wednesdays and Thursdays 10–3 and weekends 12–6), so is the adjacent **snack bar.** But whether you bring or purchase food, you'll find enough picnic tables and wide-open spaces here to accommodate scores of families.

Not nearly as glitzy, large, or crowded as the Smithsonian's National Air and Space Museum, this NASA-run museum, called the Visitor Center, brings space flight down to earth while letting imaginations soar. Though the center wasn't designed specifically for children, even toddlers are amused by the many buttons and earphones that accompany the exhibits.

Among the real spacecraft on display is the compact car–size *Gemini XII* capsule, where astronauts Buzz Aldrin and Jim Lovell spent four days. But it's the replica of the *Gemini XII* that really excites youngsters, because they can go inside and play with 100 buttons and knobs (count them!). Press a black button and you hear the famous countdown to takeoff.

After a trip aboard the *Gemini,* kids may want to design their own satellites and rocket systems at computer stations. The computers provide all sorts of information about building rockets and will even alert you if you're over budget. (Those not as directly interested in space might prefer the Earth Science Gallery, where interactive computer kiosks explore

EATS FOR KIDS Check out the display of fast food for space flight. Then to taste the real thing, purchase astronaut's freeze-dried ice-cream sandwiches in foil pouches at the gift shop. It sounds more exciting than it is; it's messy and not particularly tasty. Picnicking is permitted on the grounds, but the only food sold here is from a vending machine. A short drive away in historic Greenbelt, the **New Deal Cafe** (113 Center Way, tel. 301/474–5642) offers a novel idea. While waiting for your soups, sandwiches, or vegetarian—even vegan— entrées, your kids can read books, play Scrabble, or work on puzzles.

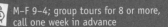 Building 88, Explorer Rd., Greenbelt, MD

 Free

M–F 9–4; group tours for 8 or more, call one week in advance

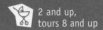 301/286–9041; www.gsfc.nasa.gov

2 and up,
tours 8 and up

climate and weather.) For children who aren't ready for computerized rocket science, Echo gives a "bat's eye" view of space during puppet shows held during the summer (check the Web site for a schedule).

Information desk volunteers are also happy to try to answer children's questions, no matter how complex or off-the-wall. For example: What kind of fuel do rockets use? Usually it's kerosene or liquid hydrogen combined with liquid oxygen in a combustion chamber. To take home a real souvenir, ask for a free lithograph of rockets and space shuttles.

Outside the center is a "rocket garden," with a real 92-foot Delta rocket and other authentic space hardware. You can also see other buildings at this sprawling government complex where scientists and engineers monitor spaceships circling the earth, the solar system, and beyond.

GETTING THERE From the Baltimore-Washington Parkway (I–295) or Capital Beltway, exit to Route 193 east (Greenbelt Road). Pass the Goddard Space Flight Center, continue ¾ mile to Soil Conservation Road, and turn left. Take the next left on Explorer Road, and follow signs.

KEEP IN MIND
Would your child like to practice reciting a countdown to takeoff or learn the basics of rocketry? On the first Sunday of each month from 1 to 2, Goddard goes overboard with outdoor rocket launches.

GREAT FALLS

Thanks to the Ice Age 2 million years ago, a wide, flat, slow-moving body of water cut its way through bedrock and created Great Falls, a lovely waterfall on the Potomac that is part of the C&O Canal National Historical Park. Here the water thrashes about faster, frothier, and noisier than the wildest bubble bath.

For information and a trail map, head to the 1831 tavern, which still welcomes visitors, though it stopped providing food and shelter in the 1930s. In the main room, a kid-level display about the canal and its locks is safely behind glass. An 1830s lock-tender's house displays an old-fashioned organ and rug beater. In the next room, a video narrated by Charles Kuralt tells about the falls, but if five minutes without animation is too long for your kids, show them the transportation exhibit instead. In 1876, horses served as cars, mules as trucks, and oxen as tractors. Their shoes are tacked to a wall, and display doors open to reveal goods carried on the canal: coal, corn, and flour.

HEY, KIDS!
Park Service rangers are the ultimate Power Rangers, preserving and protecting our country's natural, cultural, and recreational resources. You can, too. Pick up a Junior Ranger Program booklet in the tavern (for ages 6–8 or 9–12) and be a towpath detective and unlock lock history.

EATS FOR KIDS As at all National Park Service sights, you may not feed the animals, but you can feed yourselves. Buy something at the **snack bar** (open March–November), a few paces north of the tavern, or bring your own picnic. Potomac Village, 3½ miles away, has two supermarkets that sell prepared foods: **Giant** (9812 Falls Rd., tel. 301/983–4246) and **Safeway** (10104 River Rd., tel. 301/983–2150). Or take off for **Flaps** (10134 River Rd., tel. 301/983–2660), where miniature airplanes float overhead and kids can order anything from pasta with butter to lobster salad.

 11710 MacArthur Blvd., Potomac, MD

 301/299-3613, 301/767-3714;
www.nps.gov/choh

 $5 vehicles, $3 per person
without vehicle, good
for 3 days for visiting
both sides of the Falls,
in MD and VA

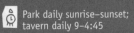 Park daily sunrise–sunset;
tavern daily 9–4:45

 4 and up

If it's hiking you're after, check out these interesting options, but beware of trails too rugged for little ones. The Billy Goat Trail sounds simple, but the 4-mile loop requires scrambling over boulders. Hiking boots and athletic ability are recommended. The Gold Mine Loop also runs about 4 miles, revealing the remains of an 1867–1939 mine. Not everyone went to California for gold. Sorry, panning isn't allowed today.

For a golden view of the falls that everyone enjoys, take the walkway to Olmsted Island. This .6-mile, wheelchair- and stroller-accessible route leads to a platform with a spectacular view of the churning waters. Along the walkway, signs alert you to ancient plants growing among the rocks. You might also see more recent arrivals: freshwater Asiatic clamshells, first reported here in the 1980s. In any case, your kids can find a cozy seat on the rocks in the middle of the platform or on the benches, and you can see Mother Nature at her wildest and wooliest.

KEEP IN MIND You can enjoy the falls from either Maryland or Virginia (9200 Old Dominion Dr., McLean, tel. 703/285-2964). The Virginia side offers more opportunities for serious rock climbers. Bring your own equipment and register at the visitor center. Swimming and wading are prohibited on both sides, but you can fish (license required for anglers 16 and older), climb rocks, or go white-water kayaking—experienced boaters and below the falls only, as currents are deadly. Despite signs and warnings, people occasionally dare the water and lose.

HIRSHHORN MUSEUM AND
SCULPTURE GARDEN

A ny child who thinks art museums only display boring, two-dimensional paintings of old-fashioned people is in for a surprise at the Hirshhorn. Here a brightly colored fish mobile made of metal and glass swims. A wet dog in bronze walks. Life-size people made of plaster ride a bus.

American artists such as Thomas Eakins, Georgia O'Keeffe, Jackson Pollock, Mark Rothko, and Frank Stella are represented along with modern European and Latin masters, including Juan Muñoz, René Magritte, and Joan Miró. The Hirshhorn's impressive collection includes one of the largest public collections of works by Henry Moore in the United States, as well as works by Willem de Kooning and others.

Okay, so most kids won't recognize or particularly care about these names. To make your museum experience fun for the inexperienced museum goer, visit the information desk for a free "Family Guide." It's full of colorful art cards that encourage your children to search

KEEP IN MIND The Hirshhorn suggests that you connect artworks with experiences meaningful to your child. When you view George Segal's *Bus Riders*, on the second floor, you could discuss where the riders might be going. Pablo Picasso's *Woman with a Baby Carriage*, also on the third floor, might elicit a story about pushing your own baby in a carriage. Although children are encouraged to get to know the art, please remind your kids not to get too friendly. The artwork is for the eyes, not the fingers.

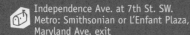 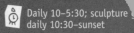

Independence Ave. at 7th St. SW.
Metro: Smithsonian or L'Enfant Plaza,
Maryland Ave. exit

Daily 10–5:30; sculpture
daily 10:30–sunset

 Free

202/357-2700, Young at Art and Improv
Art 202/633-3382; www.Hirshhorn.si.edu

 5 and up, Young at
6–9, Improv Art 5–1

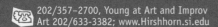

for a work, learn something about it, think about it, and relate it to their own lives and imagination. For example, on the card about Claes Oldenburg's *Geometric Mouse: Variation 1, Scale A,* kids are challenged to wonder what it would be like to be a geometric mouse visiting a mouse house with 500 other geometric mice. To design a tour for your family, allow your kids to choose their own art cards and go to the youngest child's selections first.

Two Saturday programs (offered sporadically, so call ahead) are especially attractive to youngsters. Young at Art allows early grade-schoolers (accompanied by an adult) to tour select exhibits and create their own contemporary art using some of the techniques or materials they've seen. Reservations are required. At Improv Art, elementary schoolkids and their parents can drop in for a few minutes or a few hours to explore the gallery with activity sheets. Families might look for hearts, for example, and then create valentines.

EATS FOR KIDS
When the Hirshhorn opened in 1974, detractors who didn't like the cylindrical architecture of the museum called it the Doughnut on the Mall. If you're looking for a doughnut or other goodie to eat, check out ideas under the (Smithsonian) Castle.

HEY, KIDS! Art here isn't only paint on canvas. Some art is made from mud, twigs, leaves, stone, light, video monitors, and even fat. What can you find? Can you find Kenneth Snelson's tall sculpture *Needle Tower* in the plaza? Get in its center, and look up. You'll see a star.

RNATIONAL SPY MUSEUM

43

Nancy Drew would love this museum. So would the Hardy Boys. And so do most kids. Whether they're eavesdropping on siblings or searching for hidden presents, kids love to spy. This museum takes the art of espionage to new levels for junior James Bonds.

Did you know there are more spies in Washington than in any other city? Crowds of curious visitors walk through metal detectors and watch a short video on espionage before winding through the exhibits. Like little moles, kids can crawl through the museum's ductwork to peek through the vents. They find larger-than-life-size silver flies on walls that transmit information to undisclosed locations.

Despite all the cool gadgetry that makes kids want to speed too quickly in hot pursuit of adventure through the museum, take your time when you see the replica of James Bond's Aston Martin sports car. Just like in the films, gadgets galore pop out.

EATS FOR KIDS It's no secret that the museum's **Spy City Cafe** (tel. 202/ 654–0995) serves killer sandwiches, wraps, salads, and a large selection of cookies from molasses ginger to white chocolate macadamia nut. To pursue predictable fare, cross the street to **Subway** (901 E St., tel. 202/ 737–3480).

KEEP IN MIND At peak times—spring and summer weekends and even some weekdays, Thanksgiving, and Christmas—the museum recommends advance tickets through Ticketmaster (www.ticketmaster.com) at least 48 hours in advance. The high-tech feel of this metallic and wood museum is particularly cool for preteens and teenagers. If you bring along a younger sibling, your child might not be only one who gets tired, as seating is limited and strollers aren't allowed in the museum (nor are food, beverages, and cameras).

800 F St. NW.
Metro: Gallery Place/Chinatown

202/393-7798;
www.spymuseum.org

$13 adults, $10 children age
5–18, free for children under 5

Daily 10–7

8 and up

Watch as people transform themselves into spies on videos that made Superman's telephone booth transition look simple. Through wardrobe changes, makeup, facial hair, and shoe inserts to make a person limp, a man and a woman transformed themselves into people their own close friends probably couldn't recognize.

While the museum offers clues and commentary on the capture of John Hanssen, Aldrich Ames, and other modern spies, a professional spy from the 12th century may draw just as much interest. In a huge glass cage, a life-size figure of a masked Ninja poses, representing the Japanese art of invisibility. Other tricks of the trade include homing pigeons with cameras, a pistol in a lipstick, and a spy kit with ropes, candles, flashlights, pliers, rubber gloves, and more. But don't worry—although your kids may pick up some new sleuthing ideas, fake mustaches won't work at their ages.

HEY, KIDS! Have you ever hidden stuff under your bed? Spies have concealed camera and film supplies in buttons, lipstick, a sunglasses case, wristwatches, chess pieces, shoes, and even a cuckoo clock. They've stored weapons in belts, pens, and false cigarettes. Although the life of a sleuth sounds exciting, for real life spies, the work can be boring but risky. You have to be careful not to blow your cover!

JEFFERSON MEMORIAL

Many children and adults may be surprised to learn that Thomas Jefferson didn't list being president as one of his greatest accomplishments. When he appraised his own life, Jefferson wanted to be remembered as the "Author of the Declaration of American Independence, of the Statute of Virginia for religious freedom, and Father of the University of Virginia."

The monument honoring the third president is the southernmost of the District's major monuments, four long blocks and a trip around the Tidal Basin from the Metro. Jefferson had always admired the Pantheon in Rome (the rotundas he designed for the University of Virginia and his own Monticello were inspired by its dome), so architect John Russell Pope drew from the same source when he designed this memorial. But even children who have never heard of Rome, not to mention Jefferson, can still enjoy one of the city's best views of the White House from the memorial's top steps.

KEEP IN MIND Every spring, Washington eagerly waits for the delicate flowers of the cherry trees to bloom (many of which are near the memorial). Park Service experts try their best to predict when the buds will pop—usually for about 10–12 days at the beginning of April. But regardless of when they flower, the weeklong National Cherry Blossom Festival (tel. 202/547–1500 for dates and information) is celebrated with the lighting of a ceremonial Japanese lantern, fashion shows, and a parade. When the weather complies and the blossoms are at their peak for the festival, Washington rejoices.

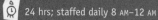
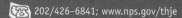

Inside the monument a 19-foot bronze statue of Jefferson on a 6-foot granite pedestal looms larger than life. And just in case your children didn't take the National Park Service ranger recommendation to research Jefferson before visiting the monument, they can learn about this Renaissance man by reading his writings about freedom and government on marble walls surrounding the statue. The whole family can take advantage of ranger programs offered throughout the day or ask questions of the ranger on duty.

An exhibit called Light and Liberty, on the lower level, provides highlights of Jefferson's life, a time line of world history during his lifetime, an etched-glass sculpture with Jefferson's words in his own handwriting, and a 10-minute video. When you've seen it all, you and your children can judge for yourselves what Jefferson's greatest accomplishments really were.

EATS FOR KIDS
A short drive away in East Potomac Park (see #51) is a golf course **snack bar** with more reasonable prices than most Mall vendors, as well as the awesome *Awakening* sculpture.

HEY, KIDS! Built during World War II, the Jefferson Memorial sparked controversy due to its cost: a then-whopping $3,192,312. Actually, the first statue erected was made of plaster, because bronze was too expensive and was needed for the war. The bronze statue you see today was not put in place until 1947.

KENILWORTH NATIONAL
AQUATIC GARDENS

41

Children like to run through this 12-acre national park devoted to aquatic plants. However, the best way to enjoy this sanctuary is to walk quietly and pause often. Hear bullfrogs croak and birds chirp, search for turtles and frogs among platter-size leaves, gaze upon exotic plants and water lilies reminiscent of a Monet painting.

Intersecting trails surround dozens of ponds filled with plants that awe and amuse, like the extraordinary South American *Victoria amazonica*, with leaves as large as a sixth grader. Ask your youngsters how cattails and yellow flag irises got their names or whether pickerelweeds and rose mallow shrubs (no relation to marshmallows) look as silly as they sound. Watch for frogs jumping onto lily pads, turtles sunbathing, and crayfish burrowing mud chimneys to escape from turtles and birds. You might see blue herons, bald eagles, and muskrats near the river, but don't restrict yourselves to sight and sound. Let your other senses, like touch and smell (tasting isn't recommended), help you explore the park, too.

EATS FOR KIDS There aren't any restaurants within walking distance of these gardens tucked away in a corner of North-east Washington, and the only food or drink available here is a water fountain at the visitor center. Instead, pack a lunch and take advantage of the picnic tables near the ponds.

KEEP IN MIND Driving directions are tricky; it's best to call ahead. If you do get lost, you should know that locals refer to Kenilworth as "lily ponds." Keep a careful eye on children, especially preschoolers, while they search for aquatic life. Although the ponds are only 3 feet deep, the banks can be slick and there are no fences around them. The only barriers are those in the ponds, designed to protect the plants. You are what protects your kids, but don't worry if their clothes get a little dirty. It's all part of the fun.

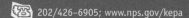

The best time to visit is 8–11, when day-bloomers are opening and night-bloomers have yet to close. Water lilies flower through the summer. Pick up maps at a tiny visitor center: one for the ponds and one for the Anacostia River trail, at whose end you can see beaver hutches at low tide. Incidentally, unlike the beavers that gnawed down cherry trees on the Mall in 1999, the Kenilworth beavers are helpful. By dining on water lilies, they keep the plants from getting too crowded to flower.

For young children, ask for a treasure list, which changes every few months. In winter, you can search for the shells of pond crustaceans left by birds and follow animal tracks. Do you think the bird got away, or did the fox eat last night? In spring, you may hunt for muskrat holes in the dikes or watch female dragonflies dip their tails in the water to lay eggs. Whatever the season, it's fun watching kids explore Kenilworth.

HEY, KIDS! Did you know frogs hibernate, living under the mud? (So please don't throw pebbles in the pond.) Did you know some people think early settlers pulled cones from the buttonbush to make buttons? Did you know water boatman bugs swim upside down on the ponds in summer? Did you know you can learn a lot of neat stuff here?

THE KENNEDY CENTER

40

The Kennedy Center looks like a place for adults in tuxedos and black dresses, and it is. But it's also a place that rolls out the red carpet for children. As the nation's performing arts center, it takes seriously its responsibility to make an eclectic calendar of top-notch performances accessible to many. One example is the dark-red Show Shuttle, which runs between the center and Foggy Bottom every 15 minutes.

More than 100 family events are held each year through the center's Imagination Celebration (late September–early May), in which actors, dancers, storytellers, musicians, and puppeteers show off for kids. The National Symphony Orchestra puts on Kinderkonzerts and family concerts. Arrive 45 minutes early before most shows and your children can beat drums, blow into a tuba, or clang cymbals.

As part of the Performing Arts for Everyone Initiative, free 1-hour performances are held nightly at 6 on the Millennium Stage (neither ticket nor reservation required). Many provide

KEEP IN MIND Cue sheets for many children's performances are available on the Kennedy Center's Web site. Not only do the cue sheets provide background information on the performers and their art, but they often give kids a list of things to look for when watching a show. If you can't catch Millennium Stage performances at the center, you can see them live every evening on the center's Web site.

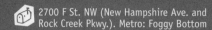 2700 F St. NW (New Hampshire Ave. and Rock Creek Pkwy.). Metro: Foggy Bottom

 Free, children's performances free–$12

Daily 10–9 (or until last show lets out); box office M–Sa 10–9, Su 12–9

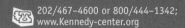 202/467–4600 or 800/444–1342; www.Kennedy-center.org

3 and up

the perfect opportunity to introduce children to classical music or opera. In others, dancers, actors, storytellers, or magicians reach out to kids of all ages. Performers have included Frank Sinatra Jr. and the Duke Ellington Orchestra, as well as local artists. Seats are generally plentiful, though kids often sit up front or on the steps, or they don't sit at all—they dance! Sometimes performers sign autographs and pose for photos. During the September open house, at least one stage is devoted to children's performances, and face painters and clowns roam the halls.

Even without seeing a performance, however, you can enjoy this six-theater memorial to President Kennedy. Pick up a "flag sheet" at the information desk, and visit the Hall of Nations and Hall of States, where the flags of more than 140 countries and all 50 states hang, the latter in order of admission to the union. Take a break on the terrace overlooking the Potomac, and watch airplanes above and boats below.

HEY, KIDS! The 618-foot-long Grand Foyer is one of the world's largest rooms. If you could lay the Washington Monument on its side in the Grand Foyer, you would still have about 3 inches to spare. Look up, and you'll see tons of crystal—literally. Each of the 18 chandeliers weighs one ton.

EATS FOR KIDS For restaurants with a view, you can't beat the top of the Kennedy Center. The **KC Café** offers self-serve soup, sandwiches, pasta salads, and pizza overlooking the Potomac and Georgetown. The formal **Roof Terrace Restaurant** isn't appropriate for most kids, but for older children with tickets to a play, it could be a great way to start the evening. Service is quick, ensuring that you get to the show on time!

LEESBURG ANIMAL PARK

W ant to get up close and personal with animals? Not only can kids talk to the animals here (the parrots will even talk back), but they can also pet and feed many of them. Domestic farm animals and exotic species live side by side at this animal park. In the contact area, llamas, goats, sheep, and even an occasional nilgai (Indian antelope) will come right up to visitors for a little affection. Kids who don't want to get too close can see and hear the animals in stalls.

Among the delights here are the antics and boisterous singing of the primates, including squirrel monkeys. Kids also enjoy kidding around with kids—baby goats, that is—who hop and jump, don't mind being petted, and love being fed. On weekends, live animal demonstrations, puppeteers, mimes, and other kids' entertainment add to the excitement.

Kids can ride ponies and go on wagon rides. Just don't expect to see any hay on the wagon—it made some people sneeze. Those who are too young to ride real animals

HEY, KIDS!

Here are some tips for interacting with the animals: when you feed one, keep your hand flat and your fingers together so they don't get accidentally nibbled along with the food. Only feed the animals what's sold at the park, because people food can make them sick. Also, remember not to shout, run, or tease the animals.

EATS FOR KIDS Goats eat just about anything—or at least try. Unlike goats, kids can be picky, and much of what they want their parents won't let them have. Snacks and candy are sold at the entrance. For a healthful alternative, bring a picnic or drive five minutes to the **Leesburg Restaurant** (9 S. King St., tel. 703/777–3292), in the middle of town. People have been filling their tummies at this dinerlike place since 1865.

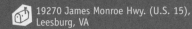 19270 James Monroe Hwy. (U.S. 15), Leesburg, VA

 703/433-0002; www.leesburganimalpark.com

 $7.50 ages 13 and up, $5.50 children 2–12; Oct $9 ages 2 and up

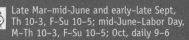 Late Mar–mid-June and early–late Sept, Th 10-3, F–Su 10–5; mid-June–Labor Day, M–Th 10–3, F–Su 10–5; Oct, daily 9–6

 1–12

can hop on plastic ones at the playground, where kids who want to play monkey head for the slides, merry-go-round, and jungle gym. Tots who dig can break ground in the sandboxes.

Birthdays are "wild" at the park, including pony rides, a live animal show, goody bags, and balloons. If you'd rather, the park will bring the zoo—four small, pettable, farmyard animals or four exotic animals, or even a customized experience—to you and your party animal.

Some kids may be concerned about the crowded conditions in some of the animal pens, but you can tell them not to be too worried. When the park closes each evening, the animals replace the children on the park's vast acreage.

KEEP IN MIND Children under 13 must be supervised, and please pay attention to the posted warnings. If a sign says an animal bites, it really does. To avoid crowds during Pumpkinville, an October festival with live entertainment, hay mazes, and, of course, pumpkins, come on a weekday afternoon.

LINCOLN MEMORIAL

Give your kids five, as in five dollars. Or give them a penny. Either way, they'll see a picture of the Lincoln Memorial. Then take them to the real thing. Many consider the Lincoln Memorial the most inspiring monument in the city, and it's also one of the most kid-friendly.

Children eager to show off newly acquired counting skills will find plenty to keep them busy here. Thirty-six Doric columns, representing the 36 states in the country at the time of Lincoln's death, surround the somber statue of the seated Lincoln. Above the frieze are the names of the 48 states of the union when the memorial was dedicated in 1922. (Alaska and Hawaii are noted by an inscription on the plaza leading up to the memorial.)

Older children may practice their oratorical skills by reciting two of Lincoln's great speeches—the Second Inaugural Address and the Gettysburg Address—which are carved on the north and south walls. Kids can even find the exact spot (look down for the engraving

KEEP IN MIND Consider bringing your kids back at night in their pajamas for a "Goodnight, Mr. Lincoln" tour, run by Washington Walks (202/484–1565; www.washingtonwalks.com), second and fourth Saturdays of the month at 7 PM (Memorial Day through Labor Day). Participants learn what kind of bed young Abe slept in, what his pajamas were like, and whether or not he brushed his teeth before bed. The tour includes playtime with Lincoln Longs and a bedtime story on why Lincoln grew a beard. Tuck-in is still up to you.

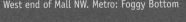

added in 2003) on the steps of the Lincoln Memorial where Martin Luther King Jr. gave his famous "I Have a Dream" speech in 1963.

Though many visitors look only at the front and interior of the monument, there is much more to explore. On the lower level, to the left of the main stairs, is Lincoln's Legacy, a display that chronicles the memorial's construction. A video and photos depict famous demonstrations and speeches that have taken place here, and another exhibit shows postage stamps from around the world that feature Lincoln on them.

If you don't need to get home for an 8:30 bedtime, come at night, one of the best times to see the memorial. (Though minimal parking is available along Ohio Drive during the day, additional parking is available in the evening along Constitution Avenue.) Spotlights illuminate the exterior, whereas inside, light and shadows play across Lincoln's gentle face.

EATS FOR KIDS
A **refreshment stand** (French Dr., north side of Independence Ave. SW) serves sandwiches, fries, chicken fingers, just a short walk from the memorial.

HEY, KIDS! The statue of Lincoln is actually composed of 28 separate pieces of marble, which were hand-carved individually and then only assembled when they arrived at the memorial chamber. The face and hands look especially lifelike because they are based on castings done of Lincoln while he was president. You might find it hard to take your eyes off them.

MADE BY YOU

37

As the explosion of craft kits on the market can attest, kids love creating their own masterpieces, and take more pride and satisfaction in making their own souvenirs and gifts than in going out and buying them (even with your money). Made By You, a paint-your-own-pottery studio, does craft kits one better.

Children choose from more than 150 items to paint, including ceramic mugs, piggy banks, animal boxes, dinosaurs, picture frames, and, of course, tiles. After the glaze dries, the ceramic pieces are fired in a kiln, and the result is a professional-looking product that's ready to be picked up in four days.

During their summer camp for ages 6–9 and 10 and up, kids engage in lots of clay play that may include creating picture frames or rolling, cutting, and painting beads. They also transform broken ceramic pieces into mosaics on 6" x 6" tiles.

HEY, KIDS!

Your ceramic master-piece will be fired in a kiln hotter than your oven at home—much hotter. Your creation will get cooked at 2,000°F. That's as hot as lava from a volcano!

EATS FOR KIDS

If after that special craft goody has been made by you and your child, you feel like an edible goody made by someone else, visit the **Firehook Bakery** (3411 Connecticut Ave. NW, tel. 202/362–BAKE[2253]). The specialties are sandwiches on fresh breads and cookies the size of a kindergartner's hands. Outdoor seating is in a beautiful garden with a fountain and an overhead trellis with hanging grape vines.

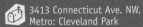
3413 Connecticut Ave. NW.
Metro: Cleveland Park

Projects $7–$60,
avg $22; camp $150

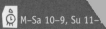
M–Sa 10–9, Su 11–

202/363–9590;
www.madebyyou.com

4 and up

Gather a group of eight or more people (children and adults), and you can arrange for your own gala here. With two weeks advance notice, the staff will help you plan a 2-hour pottery-painting party for your birthday child or scout troop. Made By You will also help with fund-raising projects. A picnic table with tiles decorated by children brought in $1,000 for one local school.

But one of the best things about craft-making at Made By You never leaves the store. Though it might get to be a bad habit if they could get away with it every day, your children won't have to clean up after themselves—but then neither will you. That dreaded chore is left to the staff. That alone, not to mention the smiles on your children's faces, can be worth the slightly pricey cost of these semi-handmade creations.

KEEP IN MIND Made By You is a challenging place to take an inquisitive toddler. There are plenty of easily accessible and easily broken items for little fingers to get into. On the other hand, many parents bring in their infants to put hand or footprints on plates. If this location isn't convenient for you, there are others in the area: in Bethesda (4923 Elm St., tel. 301/654–3206) and Rockville, Maryland (209 N. Washington St., tel. 301/610–5496), and Arlington, Virginia (2319 Wilson Blvd., tel. 703/841–3533).

56

A visit to Mount Vernon offers much more than a chance to see George Washington's elegant and stately mansion. Depending on the time of year, kids may ride wagons, sample hoecakes cooked over an open fire, hike nature trails, learn songs that slaves sang, or observe the heritage breeds of farm animals that lived here long ago.

Tours of Washington's home and three gardens are self-guided. Historic interpreters throughout the house answer questions and give you a sense of the country's first president. Be sure to tell your children to look up on the ceiling in the first room to find pictures of farm tools. Upstairs, the beds may look small, but that's an optical illusion resulting from their being high off the ground. The shortest mattress is 6'3", a tad longer than the general himself. Perhaps more interesting to kids than the house are a dozen meticulously restored outbuildings, including a major greenhouse, a kitchen, stables, and slave quarters.

HEY, KIDS! Did you know that George Washington is the only U.S. president who did not live in the White House? During Washington's administration, the nation's capital was first in New York and then in Philadelphia. He oversaw the creation of Washington, D.C., including the White House, but never lived there. For more Washington trivia, write to the Mount Vernon Education Department (Box 110, Mount Vernon, VA 22121) for a free copy of the brochure "Rare Facts. Curious Truths."

South end of George Washington
Memorial Pkwy., Mt. Vernon, VA

$11 ages 12 and up,
$5 children 6–11

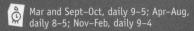
Mar and Sept–Oct, daily 9–5; Apr–Aug,
daily 8–5; Nov–Feb, daily 9–4

703/780-2000;
www.mountvernon.org

4 and up

From Memorial Day to Labor Day, the Hands-on History tent (open daily 10–1) lets kids learn about 18th-century life the old-fashioned way. They can card and spin wool, construct wooden buckets, dress in period clothing, play hoops, and harness a fiberglass mule named Nelly. They can even crawl into a Revolutionary War tent full of soldiers' gear and see how they measure up to a life-size likeness of the 6'2", 190-pound Washington.

From April 1 to Thanksgiving, kids get a feel for Colonial farm life at the George Washington: Pioneer Farmer site, which has a full-size reproduction of Washington's 16-sided barn. Depending on the day's activities, youngsters may crack corn, build a fence, hoe the fields, or dig for real potatoes. Special events include sheep shearing in May and plowing in June. No matter what time of year you visit Mount Vernon, pick up an Adventure Map. The real treasure is that kids learn about the father of our country.

KEEP IN MIND
Mount Vernon is the second-most-popular historic home in the country. (The White House is the first.) Tourists pull up by the busload in spring and summer. To beat the crowds, arrive in the early morning or at around 3, but remember that the grounds close at 5.

EATS FOR KIDS To protect Mount Vernon from damage and litter, food and beverages are not permitted on the grounds. Just outside the main gate you'll find a **food court pavilion** with indoor and outdoor seating. For a taste of Colonial life, try Colonial Turkey Pye or peanut and chestnut soup at the **Mount Vernon Inn** (tel. 703/780–0011). The inn also offers modern meals, such as chicken fingers and hamburgers for kids.

MYSTICS BASKETBALL

Kids don't need a wizard's wand or sorcerer's stone to enjoy the magic of the Mystics, Washington's popular WNBA team. Adults don't need a wad of money either. At a fraction of what it costs to watch the Wizards (Washington's NBA team), you can catch a family-friendly Mystics game at the MCI Center, the 20,000-seat arena at the crossroads of Metro's red, green, and yellow lines.

Women have come a long way since they first dribbled basketballs in 1892, a year after the game was invented and nearly three decades before they won the vote. People could have hardly imagined a women's professional basketball league back in the early 1890s, when women wore floor-length dresses, even on the court. They gained more freedom in 1896, when they began playing in bloomers, loose-fitting trousers gathered at the knee. Now, of course, they, like men, dress for comfort and ease of motion when they play, sweating through plenty of socks (around 960!) each season.

KEEP IN MIND Gather a group of 20 or more and you not only qualify for discount tickets, you can have your group's message, such as "Happy Birthday" or "Congratulations," highlighted on the telescreen. You don't even need to plan far in advance. A day's notice (tel. 202/661–5050) is all you need!

HEY, KIDS! If you ever come for a Capitals game, you might want to visit the Hockey 101 booth, where team representatives answer your questions. For example, how many sticks do the players use? Some players may go through a couple per game, while others use one for a whole season. How do players sharpen their skates? They don't. The equipment manager sharpens them. If you're too young to ask questions, ask for a hug from Slapshot, the Capitals' mascot. With a wingspan of 6', this eagle can tickle you with his feathers.

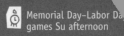 Memorial Day–Labor Da[y]
games Su afternoon

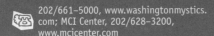 601 F St. NW. Metro: Gallery Place/Chinatown

202/661–5000, www.washingtonmystics.
com; MCI Center, 202/628–3200,
www.mcicenter.com

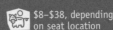 $8–$38, depending
on seat location

 5 and up

The crowds go wild as the royal-blue, gold, and white–clad Mystics prove with each shot that they got game. A royal-blue rabbit named Charm; her cohort, Mini-Charm; and 25 Mayhem dancers, ages 7–18, cheer on the players and spread high-fives through the crowd. (Just think: 600 kids try out for the Mayhem.) During half-time, kids wearing Mystics uniforms (including shoes) join the Mayhem for Dress and Dribble. Alternatively, fans are encouraged to don Hawaiian attire for Beach Night; sombreros for Salsa Night; and red, white, and blue for Spirit of America day. At the Mystics' sleepover party, kids bring sleeping bags for a night of movies and games (one parent per child).

For a time-out during the game, head to the FanZone, where kids can measure their hands and feet against those of the Mystics' Courtney Alexander and the Wizards' Michael Jordan and Richard Hamilton. Need another reason to see the Mystics? Tickets are easier to come by than for the MCI Center's other teams, the Wizards and Capitals of the NHL.

EATS FOR KIDS Eat at the game or stroll under the gold and red arch to Chinatown. Children pat Buddha's tummy before filling their own at **Hunan Chinatown** (624 H St. NW, tel. 202/783–5858). **Tony Cheng's** (619 H St. NW, tel. 202/371–8669) offers barbecue on the first floor and traditional fare upstairs.

many

34

There's a good reason why this place is the most popular museum in the world: Kids love it. The 23 galleries here tell the story of aviation and space from the earliest human attempts at flight. Suspended from the ceiling like plastic models in a child's room are dozens of aircraft, including the actual Wright 1903 Flyer that Orville Wright piloted over the sands of Kitty Hawk, Charles Lindbergh's *Spirit of St. Louis,* the X-1 rocket plane in which Chuck Yeager broke the sound barrier, and the X-15, the fastest plane ever built.

Kids like walking through the backup model of the *Skylab* orbital workshop to see how astronauts live (in quarters as cramped as a child's messy bedroom). At the How Things Fly gallery, children sit in a real Cessna 150 cockpit, "perform" experiments in midair, and see wind-tunnel demonstrations. An activity board at the gallery entrance lists times for such family favorites as Flights of Fancy storytelling (ages 3–7), paper airplane contests, and demonstrations by museum "Explainers," high school and college students who encourage kids to participate. At the newest exhibit, Explore the Universe, kids learn how

EATS FOR KIDS Take your place in the **cafeteria** line for a bite of the most familiar restaurant food on earth—McDonald's—plus offerings from Boston Market and Donatos Pizza. Upstairs you can look out on the U.S. Capitol, the Mall, and the National Gallery of Art and Sculpture Garden. If you want a treat to take home, head to one of the three gift shops, which sell such flight-related merchandise as freeze-dried astronaut food.

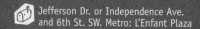

past stargazers mapped the heavens with telescopes, cameras, and spectroscopes and what mysteries about our universe still remain.

Don't let long lines deter you from seeing a show in the five-story Samuel P. Langley Theater. IMAX films like *To Fly!* (a kids' favorite) make you feel you've left the ground. Strollers aren't allowed at the movies, but then kids under 4 may find the noise and larger-than-life images frightening anyway.

For a look at the final frontier, check out the Albert Einstein Planetarium. *Infinity Express,* a 20-minute tour of the universe, is shown throughout the day. *The Stars Tonight,* for stargazers 6 and up, discusses at noon what you can expect to see that night. Films and planetarium shows sell out quickly, so buy tickets upon arrival (or in advance). You can also touch the moon rock (at the Mall exit) one of only three on the planet you can feel.

HEY, KIDS! You're one in a million . . . Make that 9 or 10 million—annual visitors, that is. The world's most popular museum is also thought to be earth's most visited building. But don't feel insignificant. Our sun may be one of many billions of stars, but look how important it is.

KEEP IN MIND The museum is large (three blocks) and popular. To avoid crowds, go early on a weekday morning. Consider dressing your children in identical colors so that you can spot them easily. Also, review safety rules ahead of time, and point out what the guards are wearing (white shirts, navy slacks, and hats) so your children know whom to turn to if they get lost.

NATIONAL AQUARIUM

The basement of the Department of Commerce building is a strange address for a tourist attraction, but that's where you'll find the world's third-oldest public aquarium. Since the 1870s, it has housed interesting sea creatures, including a two-headed diamond terrapin in the 1940s, whose two heads would compete for the same morsel of food. Although you won't see any two-headed creatures or huge sharks that make a big splash, this museum's small size is a plus for parents of tots.

Unlike more modern aquariums, this one is small enough that you can circle through it in about 20 minutes. Aisles are wide enough for double strollers, and the aquarium isn't generally crowded. Nevertheless, more than 250 species and 1,700 specimens of aquatic life, including American alligators, spiny lobsters, flashlight fish, clownfish, flesh-chomping piranhas, and their seaworthy mates swim here. Animals live in traditional numbered rectangular tanks. In the touch pool, kids can handle horseshoe crabs, hermit crabs, and whelks, snails the size of six-year-old's palm.

KEEP IN MIND If this National Aquarium whets your appetite for fish, visit Baltimore's glitzier National Aquarium (Pier 3, tel. 410/576–3800; www.aqua.org). An hour's drive from D.C. off-peak, it's Maryland's top tourist attraction. But be warned: It's more expensive and crowded than Washington's aquarium.

HEY, KIDS! Things aren't always what they seem. The horseshoe crab isn't really a crab at all. It's more closely related to a spider. And the green moray eel is actually blue with a yellow coating that protects it from disease and infection. But one thing is as it appears. A moray's menacing-looking mouth does deliver a very fierce bite. Fans of *Finding Nemo* may find it neat that clownfish are immune to the stings of sea anemones.

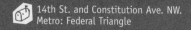 14th St. and Constitution Ave. NW.
Metro: Federal Triangle

 $3.50 ages 11 and up,
$1 children 2–10

 Daily 9–5

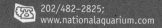 202/482–2825;
www.nationalaquarium.com

 2 and up

Challenge your child to guess the number one polluter of the Eastern shoreline from the exhibit on International Coastal Cleanup. (*Hint*: It's not good for people either.)

Special events are held throughout the year. On Shark Day, you can watch a shark dissection. During Reptile Day, herpetologists (reptile experts) rave about these cold-blooded vertebrates. Did you know that American alligators have 80 cone-shape teeth that they lose twice a year until they stop growing? They keep the tooth fairy—or shall we say tooth fish—busy!

The aquarium lost government funding in 1982 and almost closed, but a group of fish-lovers formed a nonprofit group to save it. Before you leave, consider dropping a donation in the box in front the shark tank to keep the aquarium afloat.

EATS FOR KIDS Sharks are fed at 2 on Monday, Wednesday, and Saturday. Piranhas are fed at 2 on Tuesday, Thursday, and Sunday. Alligators are fed at 2 on Friday. People can catch a bite to eat at any time at food courts in the lower level of the **Ronald Reagan Building** (1300 Pennsylvania Ave. NW, tel. 202/312–1300). On a pleasant day, consider walking over to the top level of **The Shops** (*see* the White House).

NATIONAL BUILDING MUSEUM

Budding builders and architects are awed by this monumental redbrick building. The Great Hall, site of many inaugural balls, is 15 stories tall and as long as a football field. Eight 75-foot Corinthian columns are among the world's largest. Though they look like marble, each is made of 75,000 bricks, covered with plaster and marbleized.

After viewing the breathtaking hall, head upstairs to the Washington: Symbol and City exhibit, where your children can handle plastic models of the Capitol, White House, Washington Monument, and Lincoln Memorial. Through interactive displays, they can create their own row houses, watch a board light up when they answer architectural questions correctly, and even choose their favorite design from among those originally submitted for the Washington Monument. Special exhibits change as often as 10 times per year, but all focus on the people, processes, or materials that create buildings and other "places." Recent exhibits have explored designing Disney theme parks, "do it yourself" home improvement, and elevators, escalators, and moving sidewalks.

EATS FOR KIDS When appetites build, visit **High Noon** (tel. 202/393–0353) in the museum for handcrafted sandwiches, salads, and desserts including Rice Krispie Treats. Eat in or take your lunch to go and sit at the benches across the street at the National Law Enforcement Officers Memorial, a tribute to officers killed in duty.

KEEP IN MIND Extensive school programs (also available to other groups, like scout troops) complement curricula in social studies, science, art, math, and history. Under the guidance of the museum's educators, students may plan an imaginary town, build model bridges, or assemble an 8' x 11' house from the ground up with foundations, wall frames, and trusses. Most programs cost a dollar or two for each student. For information, call the museum's education department. For building supplies for kids to take home, check out the museum shop.

401 F St. NW. Metro: Judiciary Square

Suggested donation $5

202/272-2448; www.nbm.org

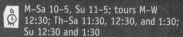M–Sa 10–5, Su 11–5; tours M–W 12:30; Th–Sa 11:30, 12:30, and 1:30; Su 12:30 and 1:30

6 and up

So why don't buildings fall down? Your children (and you) can learn why at the free, drop-in program Arches and Trusses: The Tension Builds, held every Sunday at 2:30. As part of the program, children participate in hands-on demonstrations, learning about compression by squeezing squishy balls and tension by stretching rubber bands. On Saturdays 2:30–3:30, kids learn about five basic bridge types and brainstorm about which one would solve a fictitious community's transportation problem. Then they build the bridge. Other family programs, which include building-block contests, making gingerbread houses, and dome construction, require reservations; some are free, and most are less than $10.

To get the most from the museum whenever you visit, pick up a free activity guide at the front desk. The guide helps kids explore the museum—the museum's largest artifact—at their own pace and includes activities that can be done here and at home.

HEY, KIDS! The Big Bad Wolf won't blow this house down! More than 15 million bricks make up this building, designed by Civil War veteran Montgomery Meigs and constructed from 1882 to 1887. Bricks protect against fire, important since the building housed the records and offices of the Pension Bureau—the agency that sent checks to disabled veterans and soldiers' widows. Outside, a 1,200-foot frieze (pronounced "freeze") depicts many military units. Can you find three ways people traveled on this decorative band?

NATIONAL CAPITAL TROLLEY MUSEUM

What small child doesn't love trains? And what small child who loves trains doesn't love trolleys? You can test this hypothesis at this combination trolley trip and museum. The 20-minute voyage covers 1¾ miles of track through a wooded area. Often, passengers see deer, fox, rabbits, and groundhogs, but kids are usually content just watching the trolley itself.

Also called streetcars, trolleys were first used in Washington, D.C., during the Lincoln administration to accommodate the influx of people during the Civil War. Early streetcars were drawn by horses, but these were replaced by cable cars and ultimately by electric cars, which skimmed quickly and smoothly along the tracks. The last Washington trolleys ran during the Kennedy administration. In fact, you might be riding in one of these last cars or in a car from another country. The museum's collection comprises 17 cars, which are all brought out on the third Sunday in April for the Cavalcade of Cars and the third Sunday in October for the Fall Open House. Both events also feature other attractions, such

KEEP IN MIND The biggest trolley trick for parents of toddlers is keeping them safely seated during the short ride. Luckily, the trolley makes one stop en route, when kids can get up and walk around. This is also when enthusiastic volunteers give brief trolley talks and answer questions. Often some of the passengers will remember riding the trolley when they were kids.

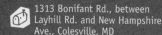 1313 Bonifant Rd., between
Layhill Rd. and New Hampshire
Ave., Colesville, MD

 $3 adults,
$2 children 2–17

 Jan–mid-Nov, Sa–Su 12–5, mid-Mar–mid-May and
early Oct–mid-Nov, Th–F 10–2 and mid-June–mid-
Aug, Th–F 11–3; Dec, Sa–Su 5–9

301/384–6088;
www.dctrolley.org

2–7 and all train lovers

as a barbershop quartet or scarecrow making. During December's Holly Trolleyfest, the museum is decked in lights, and Santa greets children during the ride.

Also take time to enjoy the museum, which resembles an old-time railroad station. Fortunately, there's no danger of losing track of your children, as the museum occupies only 1,500 square feet. With a boost, even the smallest child can press a button sending a model trolley whizzing around in a case depicting Connecticut Avenue in the early 1930s. Older kids and parents can learn the parts of a trolley and the history of D.C. trolleys through interactive computers.

Trolley memorabilia, *Thomas the Tank Engine* books, and other train-related merchandise are available in the shop. A free "Little Folks Guide to the Trolley Museum" handout and the trolley tickets themselves make nice mementos that can be used to play trolley at home.

EATS FOR KIDS
Food and drink aren't allowed in the museum or on the cars, but there are picnic tables behind the museum. Families can be choosy at the Layhill Shopping Center (Layhill and Bel Pre Rds.), where they'll find Italian fare and video games at **Sole d' Italia** (tel. 301/598–6660) and Chinese food at **Lee's Kitchen** (tel. 301/598–4810).

HEY, KIDS! Each conductor had a hole punch with a different shape—perhaps a star or zigzag. That way if a passenger complained, the conductor who punched the ticket could be identified. Today's operators still have different shape punches. What do the ones on your ticket look like?

NATIONAL GALLERY OF ART
AND SCULPTURE GARDEN

Some kids think it looks like a bird, others a plane, but most agree it's super. Looming as large as a small aircraft, a mobile by Alexander Calder soars overhead in the East Building atrium here. It's just one of the works that fascinates kids at this art museum, one of the world's most visited. The gallery comprises two very different buildings and a sculpture garden. The airy and spacious East Building's modern art—by Picasso, Matisse, Miró, and others—appeals to children, as does the exterior of the I. M. Pei–designed trapezoidal structure. In fact, since its 1978 opening, the bladelike southwest corner has been darkened and polished smooth by thousands of hands irresistibly drawn to touch it.

In the neoclassical West Building, more than 100 galleries contain 13th- to 19th-century works. Though art lovers easily spend all day here, most little children last about an hour. (Strollers are available at both buildings' entrances.) Students of architecture may notice that the building's dome shape resembles the Jefferson Memorial. Both buildings were designed by John Russell Pope and opened in the early 1940s.

HEY, KIDS!

Check out the sculpture garden's massive *Spider* by Louise Bourgeois. It's large enough to frighten even the bravest Miss Muffet. Next, find the rabbit *Thinker on a Rock*, by Barry Flanagan. Does it look like other famous rabbits? What do you suppose it's thinking about?

EATS FOR KIDS

The gallery offers several options: **On the Concourse,** a buffet, serves pizza, sandwiches, tacos, and more. The **Espresso Bar** sells light snacks and sweets. In the West Building, the **Garden Cafe** (tel. 202/216–2494; reservations recommended) features American fare. The East Building's **Terrace Café** (open Sa–Su, mid-Sept–early Jan) overlooks the Mall and the huge Calder mobile. Or why not pick up a pizza or sandwich outside at the sculpture garden's **Pavilion Café** and sit on one of the camel-back sofas?

 4th St. and Constitution Ave. NW.
Metro: Judiciary Square, Archives,
Smithsonian

 Free

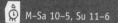 M-Sa 10-5, Su 11-6

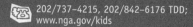 202/737-4215, 202/842-6176 TDD;
www.nga.gov/kids

 4 and up

In 1999, the gallery opened a dynamic sculpture garden with 17 works of contemporary art spread around a reflecting pool and fountain that transforms into an ice rink in winter. The only sculpture kids (or adults) can touch is Scott Burton's *Six-Part Seating,* with its polished granite chairs. Still, the meandering paths reveal unexpected treasures. Kids like to look through the window of Roy Lichtenstein's *House I.* Claes Oldenburg and Coosje van Bruggen's mammoth *Typewriter Eraser, Scale X* will look foreign to kids born in the computer age. Ask your kids to guess what it is.

Yes, visiting here will reassure you that you're exposing your children to sophisticated art and architecture and hopefully spark an interest in them. But don't be surprised if the highlight of their experience is tossing pennies into the sculpture garden's fountain or riding the moving walkway in the underground tunnel connecting the two buildings.

KEEP IN MIND Free weekend Family Workshops (registration required; call up to 3 weeks in advance) include tours and activities. Some programs, such as Stories in Art, are for children as young as 4. If you'd rather go it alone, start in the Micro Gallery to preview works by computer and print a personalized map. You may also borrow a Family Postcard Tour from the East Building's front desk, purchase a "Family Guide" ($2.50) from the Children's Shop, or rent the Adventures in Art family audio tour, which explores Dutch and Flemish paintings, in the Rotunda ($3 per tour, $2 for extra headphones, ages 7–12).

NATIONAL GEOGRAPHIC'S
EXPLORERS HALL

The National Geographic Society's famous yellow-bordered magazine—found in doctors' offices, family rooms, and attics nationwide—is not exactly for kids. Yet Explorers Hall brings the planet's wonders closer and shows kids that it is indeed a small world after all.

Inside, you can look into the crevices of a model of the Grand Canyon about the size of a dining room table and the windows of a Bathysphere, a spherical steel diving chamber that some kids say looks like a UFO. The chamber took two men down more than 3,000 feet to observe the bottom of the ocean in 1934. Kids can also smile for the camera and put their faces on the cover of the National Georgraphic. Postcard-size pictures ($5) can be made at In the Picture, where they can choose their own backgrounds—among the tulips outside the White House, on Mount Everest, next to penguins, or on the moon.

Most exhibits rotate just as the moon and earth do. Past displays have explored crawling through a coral reef, a school-bus size skeletal cast of a crocodile that lived during

KEEP IN MIND You're free to roam through the museum on your own, but if you have any questions—about the exhibits or the society—look for a docent. They wear navy blazers with globes on the pockets. Or ask at the information desk. While you're in the M Street lobby, be sure to look up at the ceiling to see stars arranged the way they were when the National Geographic Society charter was signed in January 1888 in Washington, D.C.

dinosaur days, models of famous ships such as the *Titanic* and Shackleton's *Endurance*.

On Passport Fridays, held about once a month, you don't need a photo ID or luggage. Just come between 10 and 12, when the society sponsors family entertainment. One Friday might bring African music; another Friday, Irish musicians. Dancers from around the world show off fancy footwork, and occasionally conservationists bring in live birds and reptiles. On pleasant days, Passport Fridays performances are held in the outdoor courtyard.

Every day of the year, 24 hours a day, you can walk outside the museum's portico and peer through the glass to see relief maps created with satellite imagery and artifacts from past expeditions. You may watch and listen to the National Geographic channel or check out the electronic ticker tape, which, not unexpectedly, tells about the latest discoveries in geography.

HEY, KIDS! Through magazines, TV, videos, maps, books, CD-ROMs, and the Internet, the National Geographic Society brings the world of geography to the whole world. Nearly 10 million magazines in 23 languages are mailed each month to people in *every* country. What would you like to know?

EATS FOR KIDS In a neighborhood catering to businesspeople, you won't find high chairs, but you will find reasonable prices. The self-service **California Grill** (1720 M St. NW, tel. 202/463–4200) specializes in Mexican and American cuisine. At the **Mudd House** (1724 M St. NW, tel. 202/822–8455), parents sip specialty coffees while kids enjoy hot chocolate.

NATIONAL MUSEUM OF AFRICAN ART

Kids can really relate to the art at this museum. Perhaps it's because every child has turned a paper plate into a mask or strung beads together to make a necklace. Perhaps it's because so many of the works incorporate animals. Wander through this Smithsonian museum with your child, and you'll see all sorts of African artworks: musical instruments, pottery, beaded works, sculptures, carvings, and masks and headdresses made to entertain or personify characters or animals. One tall mask from Zaire, for example, is made of painted woods and raffia (plant fiber) and was worn at rituals celebrating the arrival of the new moon. Jewelry on display is made of such materials as beads, woods, fiber, bronze, ivory, and fired clay.

One of the best ways to learn about the arts and cultures of Africa is through the AfriKid Art programs, aimed at kids 4 and up. At drop-in workshops (most of which are free), children are taught about the materials, colors, animals, and countries of origin of items in the permanent collection, such as a colorful beaded crown or a life-size figure of a man.

EATS FOR KIDS The National Air and Space Museum, the National Museum of Natural History, and the National Museum of American History have on-site restaurants (*see* listings).

HEY, KIDS! Create your own African treasure hunt. Find the pipe carved into a train. Hunt down a bird perched on an ivory spoon or the African "pillow"—actually a carved wooden headrest shaped like an elephant—and decide if it looks comfortable. What about the enormous hammered gold earrings, which are frequently supported by a leather strap? If you need help finding any items, ask at the information desk.

950 Independence Ave. SW.
Metro: Smithsonian

Free

Daily 10–5:30

4 and up

202/357–4600, 202/357–4814 TDD;
www.si.edu/nmafa

They may also be asked to answer questions like, "How would you describe the object to someone who couldn't see it?" or "How do you think it would feel to wear this hat?" After touring the gallery, kids pursue an activity, such as beading, weaving, or hat making, and can take their masterpiece home as a souvenir.

To help in your exploration, consider counting the number of equestrian figures in the gallery or imagining what your child would see beyond the large palace door.

The museum also has storytelling sessions, during which folktales are often combined with music and dance to bring legends from the African continent to life. And in the true tradition of African storytelling, the audience frequently chimes in.

KEEP IN MIND To expand your children's global view even further, walk about 100 paces west through the Enid A. Haupt Garden or just open the door at the end of the Art of the Personal Object gallery, and you'll be in the Sackler Gallery (see #14), which is connected to the Freer Gallery of Art. The emphasis at these nearby museums is on another continent altogether: Asia.

n you see the flag that inspired "The Star-Spangled Banner," Oscar the Grouch, riginal teddy bear from 1903, first ladies' inaugural gowns, and a five-story use? You can, and you can see lots more American memorabilia at three floors of mibitions, whose incredible diversity of artifacts gave it the nickname "the nation's attic."

Exhibits on the first floor emphasize the history of science and technology and include farm machines, antique automobiles, and a 260-ton steam locomotive. Two *Jurassic Park* eggs and an orange-masked Teenage Mutant Ninja Turtle are in the Science in American Life exhibit. The second floor, devoted to U.S. social and political history, has an exhibit on everyday American life after the Revolution. It even contains a house. Within These Walls follows the lives of families who lived at 16 Elm Street in Ipswich, Massachusetts, from the mid-1760s through 1945. The third floor's Icons of American Pop Culture displays familiar items, from Dorothy's ruby slippers in the *Wizard of Oz* to Michael Jordan's Bulls jersey from the 1996 NBA finals to Indiana Jones's jacket and hat. The floor also features

HEY, KIDS! Have you ever worked on a laptop? In the American Presidency: A Glorious Burden, you can see the portable wooden lap desk that Thomas Jefferson designed and used to draft the Declaration of Independence. Also check out George Washington's sword and Abraham Lincoln's top hat. If you'd rather speak than see, you can recite excerpts from famous speeches by Franklin Roosevelt, John F. Kennedy, and Ronald Reagan. You choose. You may not attract as much attention as these former presidents, but visitors to the museum will stop and listen to you. They may even applaud.

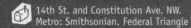 14th St. and Constitution Ave. NW.
Metro: Smithsonian, Federal Triangle

 Free

 Daily 10–5:30; Hands On History T–Su 12–3;
Hands On Science T–F 12:30–5, Sa–Su 10–5

 202/357–2700;
www.americanhistory.si.edu

2 and up, Hands On
History 5 and up, Hands
On Science 5 and up

money, graphic arts, musical instruments, photography, and news reporting.

For a more interactive visit, children and adults should stop at two places: In the Hands On History Room, you can straddle a high-wheeler, send messages by telegraph, gin cotton, and say hello in Cherokee. In the Hands On Science Center, kids project lasers to measure distance, unravel the mysteries of DNA, conduct tests for water pollutants as scientists did in the 1880s, and become "Star-Spangled Banner" conservators.

Request one of the free "Hunt for History" guides for ages 6–9 and 10–13, at an information desk. The "Peanuts" characters take children on a scavenger hunt throughout the museum. Older kids may appreciate more detailed information in free postcards. Both guides and postcards are available in English and Spanish.

EATS FOR KIDS
If your kids scream for ice cream, visit the museum's Victorian era–inspired **Ice Cream Parlor.** If they save room, two or more children might want to share a huge banana split. For other options, the **Main Street Café,** on the lower level, serves all-American barbecue, sandwiches, salad, and pizza, plus German and Italian fare.

KEEP IN MIND If you bring a purse or other bag with you, allow a little extra time for security. During busy times, both hands-on rooms require passes, which let you stay ½ hour. The free passes are available on a first-come, first-served basis at the door to each room. Adults must accompany children to hands-on rooms and the presidential exhibit, so plan on learning along with your kids.

NATIONAL MUSEUM OF THE
AMERICAN INDIAN

Your introduction to American Indian life and indeed U.S. history begins before you enter the newest Smithsonian museum. Plants that were native to the land before European settlers came grow in an upland hardwood forest, lowland freshwater wetlands, and a meadow. Crops known as the "three sisters"—corn, beans, and squash—will also grow. Cascading water represents purification and a nurturing spirit. Even the building's stone-clad forms reflect the wearing of wind and time.

Above the information desk, look and listen as the words and sounds at the Welcome Wall come from languages of Native people from the northern tip of the Arctic to the southern tip of South America. Then feel the cool copper bands woven into the wall representing traditions of textiles and basketry. Throughout the day, Native artisans will build boats with wood, braided twine, and even seal skin in the traditions of their ancestors. Not only will the boat makers demonstrate their craft, they'll also answer questions. No matter when you arrive, look at the "light show" reflected from the prism window. When the

HEY, KIDS!
The boulders outside of the museum are known as "grandfathers," because they are so old, they represent Native peoples' ancestors. Many Native peoples believe that the rocks represent living spirits. The museum's boulders are at least a billion years old.

EATS FOR KIDS Watch salmon being cooked over a fire pit built into the floor of the museum's **Mitsitam Café**. Mitsitam means "Let's Eat" in the language of the Delaware and Piscataway. While your kids may not care for salmon, they probably like popcorn. Choose from food native to five geographic regions: Northern Woodlands, South America, Northwest Coast, Meso-American, and the Great Plains. Whatever region's cuisine you select, try to get a seat at the window where it looks as if the water outside disappears under your feet.

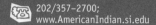

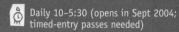

sun is at its peak, from 11 AM to 2 PM, the sun's beams dance across the floors and walls.

Check out the floor-to-ceiling cases along the walls of the Window on Collections' exhibits. Challenge your child to find the walrus head made out of motorcycle parts and the toy buffalo made from buffalo hide.

The museum also helps explore old cultural myths. You've heard of cowboys and Indians. Well, some Native Americans were cowboys and cowgirls, too. They ranched and entertained folks with their rodeo skills. Even children who have studied American Indians may be surprised to learn that more died from diseases brought from European settlers than from wars.

Even kids too young to appreciate history will enjoy the sights and sounds of native bead workers, weavers, drummers, storytellers, and dancers at the museum's indoor and outdoor theaters.

KEEP IN MIND The museum's gift shop carries an impressive collection of books for children about Native American life, from the lovely legends of yesteryear to life today to folklore fantasies. In *Coyote in Love with a Star*, the famous trickster takes a job as a rodent control officer at the former World Trade Center in New York City. Through the "My World" series, kids meet real Native American children. You can also pick up some authentic native crafts at reasonable prices.

NATIONAL MUSEUM OF HEALTH
AND MEDICINE

Boys and girls who want real goose bumps or who have an interest in a medical career can find lots of really cool stuff at this medical museum that depicts the fight against injury and disease. Because some of the exhibits are fairly graphic (e.g., wax surgical models, organs in formaldehyde), the museum may not be suitable for the squeamish.

At the Pregnancy exhibit, kids can put on a garment that makes them appear pregnant and can then attempt to tie their shoes, perhaps instilling some small appreciation for what their mother went through. At the Human Body exhibit, they can get an up-close look at human organs, like livers, stomachs, lungs, and kidneys. Some organs are "plastinated"—preserved in plastic so they can be touched—and injected with blue and red dyes so arteries can be distinguished from veins. All are real.

At still other exhibits, your children can learn about the evolution of the microscope, view the human body from a 3-D perspective at an interactive computer station, discover why

HEY, KIDS! Talk about a bizarre story. During the Battle of Gettysburg, a 12-pound cannonball splintered the right leg of Civil War General Daniel E. Sickles. After it was amputated, he sent the leg to this museum, then known as the Army Medical Museum, where it's still on display, along with a picture of the general as an amputee. Incidentally, the eccentric General Sickles used to visit his leg here and would sometimes bring friends to see it.

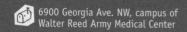 6900 Georgia Ave. NW, campus of
Walter Reed Army Medical Center

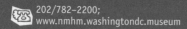 202/782-2200;
www.nmhm.washingtondc.museum

 Free

 Daily 10–5:

 9 and u

disease killed more soldiers than bullets during the Civil War, and look at early medical instruments used in skull surgery. There's much here to make everyone grateful for modern medicine. Take a look at the leeches, which were used centuries ago to treat diseases. Actually, some hospitals still use them.

Teens may view a video made by their peers about HIV testing and then test their own knowledge of HIV and AIDS, using computer games. And even if the museum's displays of how our bodies work don't get your youngsters interested in medicine, they may at least be encouraged—or even frightened—into taking steps to maintain or improve healthful habits.

EATS FOR K
For great selection and prices, walk to the **Walter Reed Hospital Cafeteria** (Bldg. 2, tel. 202/782–3501). For seafood served in a casual atmosphere, **Crisfield** (8012 Georgia Ave., Silver Spring, tel. 301/589–1306) is the place to go.

KEEP IN MIND Docents lead tours of the museum on the second and fourth Saturdays of every month at 1. Tours last 1–1½ hours and are recommended for ages 11 and up. Most docents focus on Civil War medicine. If you call ahead, the docents will bring out plastinated organs for you to feel. To keep *your* organs healthy, many docents share a tip unknown to Civil War physicians, who spread a lot of germs: Wash your hands.

...AL MUSEUM OF
NATURAL HISTORY

...ello to Henry. One of the largest elephants ever found in the world, this stuffed ...t has greeted generations of kids in the rotunda of this huge museum, which is ...d to natural wonders of the world, both big and small. From the marble floor of ...rotunda, you can look up at signs announcing the exhibits and decide where you want to go.

In the popular Dinosaur Hall, fossilized skeletons range from a 90-foot-long diplodocus to a tiny *Thesalorsaurus neglectus* (so named because its bones sat for years in a museum drawer before being reassembled). Cross the Rotunda (from the Dinosaur Hall) to the new Hall of Mammals that features 274 creatures, including lions and tigers and bears, plus more exotic animals from the Australian tree kangaroos to a South American fairy armadillo. You can meet the animals in a variety of environments—polar, desert, rainforest, and grassland.

HEY, KIDS!
In the insect zoo, you'll see ants that cut leaves, beetles that spray their enemies, and roaches that freak out grown-ups. Believe it or not, though, in some parts of the world people eat insects. Grasshoppers are the most commonly consumed, but wasps have the most protein.

KEEP IN MIND
Children explore with their hands in the Discovery Room. In the Discovery Center, you'll find the 487-seat Samuel C. Johnson Theater and its IMAX films. For 3-D flicks, you get to don oversize glasses. You won't need glasses to see the dinosaur hall's triceratops, on the first floor. Scientists studied this massive herbivore (plant eater) by scanning bones and using computers to make a lifelike cast and video. Kids can compare it to what scientists thought the triceratops looked like in 1905.

Constitution Ave. and 10th St. NW.
Metro: Smithsonian

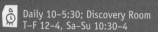 Free

Daily 10–5:30; Discovery Room
T–F 12–4, Sa–Su 10:30–4

 202/357–2700; www.nmnh.si.edu

2 and up, Discovery Room
4 and up

Older children may enjoy the Janet Annenberg Hooker Hall of Geology, Gems & Minerals, which takes rock collecting to new heights and includes a neat exhibit on volcanoes and earthquakes. The Hope Diamond is also here, slowly rotating in a four-sided glass case. The most-visited museum object in the world, it's even more popular than the *Mona Lisa*.

Not everything in the museum is dead or inanimate, though. For some action, take your kids to the second floor's O. Orkin Insect Zoo, home to live ants, bees, centipedes, tarantulas, roaches as large as mice, and other critters you wouldn't want in your house. After viewing these creepy creatures, young bug fanciers can act the part by crawling through a model of an African termite mound.

From tiny to tremendous, the natural wonders at this natural history museum will amuse your own little wonder and you.

EATS FOR KIDS Tarantula feedings take place in the insect zoo at 10:30, 11:30, and 1:30 Tuesday through Friday and 11:30, 12:30, and 1:30 on weekends. (Check at the information desk in the rotunda for a schedule.) Whereas the tarantulas' meal plan consists of the same old thing every day (crickets), you have lots of choices in the museum's 600-seat **Atrium Café** and the **Fossil Café**, where you eat at tables with little fossilized artifacts and illustrations under glass.

NATIONAL MUSEUM OF WOMEN IN THE ARTS

Every day is International Women's Day at this beautifully restored 1908 Renaissance Revival building, showcasing works by prominent female artists from the Renaissance to the present. Ironically, it was once a men-only Masonic temple. Today, in addition to traveling shows, the museum houses a permanent collection, including paintings, drawings, sculpture, prints, and photographs by such artists as Mary Cassatt, Frida Kahlo, Gabrielle Münter, and Helen Frankenthaler.

As at many art museums, it's not easy to know what children will like. Frida Baranek's nonobjective sculpture has kids talking. Some youngsters think this untitled work looks like a bird's nest or a huge tumbleweed that moves, albeit subtly. Others say it reminds them of a bad-hair day. Nineteenth-century French artist Rosa Bonheur is known for imaginative animal paintings, filled with rich and realistic textures. Teens may enjoy contrasting their practical clothes (some more practical than others) with the ornate Renaissance-era clothing of the young woman in Lavinia Fontana's *Portrait of a Noblewoman* (1580).

KEEP IN MIND Once a year, the museum is transformed from formal to fun as women and men, girls and boys gather here for music, dancing, hands-on crafts, storytelling, and more at the museum's annual Family Festival. Usually celebrating another culture, the event is generally held in early spring, but the date varies because the festival is tied in with special exhibits. By October, the museum staff should be able to tell you when the next Family Festival will be held.

 1250 New York Ave. NW.
Metro: Metro Center

202/783–5000;
www.nmwa.org

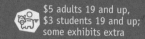 $5 adults 19 and up,
$3 students 19 and up;
some exhibits extra

 M–Sa 10–5, Su 12–5

 6 and up

Free family programs for children and role-model workshops for teens are held about once a month. Reservations are required for most programs. If you're not attending a children's program, stop by the Education Gallery to learn more about special exhibits and works from the permanent collection. From early June through mid-September, you can see artwork created by kids through the museum's Bridging Communities program. To find out how the kids made such a cool masterpieces, watch the short video of them at work.

At the information desk, pick up an "Artventure" brochure (ages 6–10), which suggests ways to look at art through the elements of line, shape, color, and texture. Even though the artists covered at the museum are limited to women, the approach to art and the appeal to visitors are universal.

HEY, KIDS! Do you like bugs? Does your mom? When Maria Sibylla Merian (born 1647) was about 14 years old, she started collecting, studying, and drawing insects. You can see Maria Merian's highly descriptive etchings and watercolors at the museum.

EATS FOR KIDS Presidential pasta and Frankenstein hot dogs are part of the draw at the **Capitol City Brewing Company** (1100 New York Ave. NW, tel. 202/628–2222). For the more adventurous eater, **Haad Thai** (1100 New York Ave. NW, tel. 202/682–1111) offers kids crispy rolls and chicken on a skewer. A bright mural set on the beaches of southern Thailand covers an entire wall.

NATIONAL POSTAL MUSEUM

L ook up and see one of the first airmail planes. Look down and see floor tiles shaped like stamped envelopes. Look around and you'll see first-class opportunities for children at this Smithsonian-operated museum dedicated to our postal history.

Six major galleries highlight such topics as the Colonial post, the Pony Express, mail transportation, and the beauty and lore of stamps. More than 40 interactive games and touch screens offer hands-on opportunities to learn more about mail. But the museum isn't all high tech. One exhibit re-creates a Native American trail that postal carriers followed between New York and Boston. There aren't any signs to guide you. The only way to find the right route is to look for notches in the trees. Another exhibit celebrates the art and history of letter writing, but even kids too young to read or write are engaged here. Youngsters can climb aboard a stagecoach, pretend to sort mail in a railway postal car, and watch videos of famous train robberies.

KEEP IN MIND This Smithsonian museum is much smaller than its cousins on the Mall. You can wander through in about 45 minutes. Consider combining a visit here with one to the Capital Children's Museum (see #63) or hop on the Metro to the Mall.

HEY, KIDS! Camels, birds, reindeer, and dogs have all helped deliver the mail, but although Owney the Dog never carried any, he was still the mascot of the railway mail service in the late 19th century. Owney logged some 143,000 miles in his career and was a genuine celebrity, making appearances at dog shows and conventions. If David Letterman had been alive, Owney would no doubt have visited the *Late Show*. Thanks to taxidermy, you can actually see Owney at the museum.

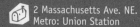

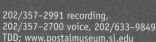

2 Massachusetts Ave. NE.
Metro: Union Station

202/357-2991 recording,
202/357-2700 voice, 202/633-9849
TDD; www.postalmuseum.si.edu

Free

Daily 10–5:30

3 and up

Families can rubber-stamp their approval on the activities at the Discovery Center, near the statue of Ben Franklin, the first U.S. postmaster. Here kids play games, hear stories, and create crafts that reflect museum exhibits or annual celebrations. In March, kids might study an Irish immigration stamp and make shamrock wands. In April, they often create hats to wear for Earth Day, and June might see them making flags to celebrate Flag Day. Come early for the best selection of materials.

When you're ready to leave the museum, make sure your children check out the customized postcard machine. After a postcard is addressed, the computer uses maps and sound to show how it will travel to its intended destination—anywhere in the world.

EATS FOR KIDS Gettysburger Address (cheeseburger), federal (chicken) fingers, and presidential pasta are on the kids' menu at the **Capitol City Brewing Company** (2 Massachusetts Ave. NE, tel. 202/842–2337), in the same building as the museum. Across the street is **Union Station** (*see* the Capital Children's Museum and D.C. Ducks), where you can choose among a huge food court and many restaurants.

NATIONAL ZOO

Known more for political animals than real animals, Washington nevertheless possesses one of the world's foremost zoos. Start with any must-see creatures on your child's list. On busy days there may be waits at the popular animal houses, such as the new Giant Panda House, Reptile Discovery Center, or Amazonia's tropical rain forest. In the Great Flight Room, birds fly unrestricted. Orangutans swing on overhead cables from the Great Ape House to the Think Tank, where you can get a good look at big apes while they get a better look at you. High-tech orangutans communicate with researchers using touch-screen computers.

Adoring fans flock to the new panda pair, who arrived in 2001 after years of negotiations with China. This playful, high-profile couple, named Tian Tian (pronounced t-YEN t-YEN and meaning "more and more") and Mei Xiang (roughly pronounced may shong and meaning "beautiful fragrance"), lives in the original pandas' renovated habitat. Zoo officials hope this bamboo-munching couple will produce babies, but for now, the new celebrities are having fun eating for up to 16 hours a day.

KEEP IN MIND The Cleveland Park Metro stop is a better choice than Woodley Park/Zoo, which leaves an uphill walk to the zoo but a downhill walk when you leave. Make sure your family wears comfortable shoes; the trek here is nothing compared to the walking you'll do over the zoo's 163 hilly acres. Rental strollers are available. Parking lots fill up in summer, so arrive early. In summer, early morning (or late afternoon) is a better time to catch animals alert; in cooler months, they're more active at midday.

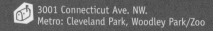
3001 Connecticut Ave. NW.
Metro: Cleveland Park, Woodley Park/Zoo

 Free

Daylight savings time grounds daily 6 AM–8 PM, animal buildings 10–6; Standard time grounds daily 6–6, animal buildings 10–4:30.

202/673–4800 or 202/673–4717;
www.si.edu/natzoo; www.fonz.org

 All ages

To see the world's fastest feline, check out the Cheetah Conservation area. To see animals with anywhere from zero to eight legs, visit the invertebrate exhibit, where octopuses, nautiluses, and giant spiders dwell. If most animals are dozing, check out the prairie dogs in the American prairie exhibit. These rambunctious rodents constantly pop in and out of their holes. Sometimes you can even hear them "bark" or make high-pitched sounds. For more barking, visit the sea lions, who perform with their pals the seals daily at 11:30.

A trip to the zoo makes for an exhausting but fulfilling day. So that everyone emerges happy and healthy, watch your kids carefully; the biggest safety problem here is not animals but children wandering off.

EATS FOR KIDS

When your tummies start to growl, get a bite at a food kiosk or at the **Mane Restaurant,** near the Bat Cave, or the **Panda Café,** near—what else—the Giant Panda House. Both restaurants serve a variety of kid-friendly food, including pizzas, burgers, sandwiches, and, of course, animal crackers.

HEY, KIDS! If you thought dragons didn't exist, check out the National Zoo's version. Though the Komodo dragons here don't fly or breathe fire, these large lizards do have scaly bodies, forked tongues, and sharp claws and teeth. Young, 6-foot Kraken, hatched in 1992, now lives in the Reptile Discovery Center.

NAVY MUSEUM

This museum is a sure bet for any child interested in things military. Just call two days ahead for a reservation and your kids can climb on cannons, operate the barrels of anti-aircraft weapons, peer through a periscope on a submarine, and even board a space capsule. All the while, they can get a maritime perspective on American history from the American Revolution to the present, including learning about the Navy's peacetime pursuits, such as diplomacy and humanitarian service. The Navy Museum is an especially good place to visit with a friend or relative who has served in the military.

Hands-on activities range from the no-tech, such as knot tying, to the high-tech, such as a Battle of Midway computer game in which children decipher coded messages. Free brochures listing activities for kids of all ages are available at the front desk. A kindergartner might do something as simple as draw a hat on a sailor or connect dots to make a plane, whereas older kids are encouraged to search for a silver sailor created from dimes or make a list of ways to prevent another world war.

EATS FOR KIDS Dine in at the Navy Yard's **Catering and Conference Center** cafeteria (tel. 202/433–3041) and familiar harbors **Subway, Dunkin' Donuts,** and **McDonald's** or take a meal to go and dine alongside seagulls at waterside picnic tables.

HEY, KIDS! Long ago, sailors as young as 9 served aboard ship, some with their fathers. During the War of 1812, Mexican War, and Civil War, quick and agile boys, called "powder monkeys," carried gunpowder from the magazine to the guns—a dangerous job, because these lads were often the targets of enemy fire. In 1755, John Barry came to America as a 10-year-old cabin boy. A.k.a. Commodore Barry (the destroyer here was named for him), he's often considered the "Father of the American Navy."

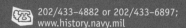 Washington Navy Yard, 11th and O Sts. SE

 Free

 Museum Apr–Labor Day, M–F 9–5; Labor Day–Mar, M–F 9–4; U.S.S. *Barry* M–F 10–4

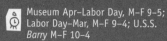 202/433–4882 or 202/433–6897; www.history.navy.mil

5 and up

If you call a few weeks in advance, you can arrange a special tour for your family or group. Themes include "Hats Off," during which kids learn about naval occupations by studying hats and then creating their own, and "To the Ends of the Earth and Beyond," in which middle-schoolers study the Navy's role in polar and underwater explorations.

Outside the museum, your family can board the decommissioned U.S.S. *Barry*, a destroyer used during the Cuban Missile Crisis and the Vietnam War. Kids like the narrow halls, bunk beds, and mess hall, but they love taking the captain's wheel to "steer" the ship. Ahoy mates!

GETTING THERE The nearest Metro stop, Eastern Market, is 15–20 minutes away, and though the Navy Yard is secure, the surrounding neighborhood isn't always safe in the evening. So especially if you're planning to stay until closing, it's best to drive. From the Beltway, take I–295 south to I–395, and follow signs to the Navy Yard.

OXON COVE PARK

19

If you want to take your children back to an era when taking care of the animals meant more than walking the family dog or feeding the cat, visit this working farm (also called Oxon Hill Farm) administered by the National Park Service. On a site where the Piscataway Indians once lived, this farm has animals and equipment typical of life in a bygone era—mostly the early 19th century and later.

Down on this farm you'll find draft horses, sheep, pigs, ducks, geese, turkeys, cows, and goats—known as poor man's cows because they're capable of eating about anything and still producing milk and cheese. Many children's favorite animal is Tuesday, the milk cow, who because she was previously a show cow, doesn't have horns. Unlike in the 19th century, most modern farmers stunt the growth of horns, as they're a hazard to farmers and other cows and they're no longer needed for protection.

EATS FOR KIDS For fresh food, bring your own and take advantage of picnic tables in the shade near the parking lot, along the path to the farm, or near the house. Otherwise, your options consist of fast-food outlets along Oxon Hill Road and the **Outback Steakhouse** (6091 Oxon Hill Rd., tel. 301/839–4300), a few miles away. Here kids can build with Legos before or after the meal and read and do puzzles while they eat.

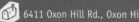 6411 Oxon Hill Rd., Oxon Hill, MD

 Free

 Daily 8–4:30

 301/839–1176; www.nps.gov/nace/oxhi

1–12

With supervision, your children can milk a cow, collect eggs warm from the nest, and—if raccoons haven't eaten it—crack and shell corn to feed the chickens. Hayrides depart afternoons at 1:30, except on Fridays when they leave at 11.

A furnished parlor in a white farmhouse owned by the DeButts family in the early 1800s is open a few times each week. Park rangers and volunteers are usually on hand to talk about the British-born Mrs. DeButts and her views on slavery and the War of 1812. Call ahead to find out when kids can participate in daily chores and when the farmhouse is open.

Oxon Hill offers free, farm-fresh programs, including sheep shearing in May, cider making in September, corn harvesting in October, and "Talking Turkey" in November. Junior ranger programs in the summertime teach 9- to 12-year-olds about farm life. Reservations for all programs are a must.

HEY, KIDS! People often think that pigs are dumb, but some farmers believe they learn more quickly than horses and dogs. One popular conception that does hold true, however, concerns their trough manners. Watch as the cows' milk is delivered to them. They eat like pigs, don't you think?

KEEP IN MIND Remind your children to move slowly near the animals and not to make any loud noises or sudden motions. Such actions are likely to startle them. And though you will no doubt get a kick out of watching your child getting a kick out of the animals, also take a moment to appreciate the panoramic view of Washington over the Potomac River.

PATUXENT NATIONAL WILDLIFE
VISITOR CENTER

18

The huge modern nature center at the Patuxent Research Refuge has enough buttons and knobs to amuse toddlers and enough gee-whiz factual information about environmental concerns to amaze teenagers. Right off the bat in the first room, older kids are challenged with such questions as "What is global warming?" and "How do we feed the world?" Younger kids may want to skip ahead to view Handles on Habitat, where they can pull a knob to see a pelican and osprey appear in the Chesapeake Bay or push a button to watch a scientist pop up with a mirror to look at birds' nests in the Hawaiian rain forest. Life-size dioramas of wild animals depict whooping cranes, timber wolves, and California sea otters swimming in kelp.

On spring–fall weekends, a 30-minute narrated tram tour runs through the refuge's meadows, forests, and wetlands, weather permitting. Though the narrator's commentary about wildlife management may be too advanced for your children, they probably will find the ride thrilling enough. Free nature movies are shown most weekends at 11, 12:30, 2, and 3:30.

HEY, KIDS!

Check out the visitor center's viewing pod. Here you can peer through binoculars and telescopes to see a lake where beavers build, birds (including an occasional bald eagle) soar, and Canada geese migrate—without even going outside.

KEEP IN MIND You may be tempted to leave most of your cash at home since, with the exception of the tram ride, all activities are free. However, bring a little money for the Wildlife Images Bookstore, which sells some interesting children's merchandise at reasonable prices. Your children might like some tattoos, stickers, rubber creatures, posters, or playing cards with pictures of endangered animals on them. Profits benefit the refuge.

10901 Scarlet Tanager Loop (off Powder · Mill Rd., between Rte. 197 and Baltimore-Washington Pkwy.), Laurel, MD

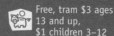 Free, tram $3 ages 13 and up, $1 children 3–12

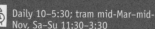 Daily 10–5:30; tram mid-Mar–mid-Nov, Sa–Su 11:30–3:30

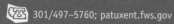 301/497–5760; patuxent.fws.gov

 2 and up

Another option is to take your own wildlife tour by following the well-marked trails. The paved Wildlife Loop is wide enough for a double stroller but short enough (about ⅓ mile) so preschoolers won't wear out. At the bird-viewing blind, even the youngest kids (with a boost from you) can peer through a slat as birds swoop within a few inches of their faces. About another 4 miles of trails, made of wood chips and other natural materials, satisfy junior and senior naturalists.

Though the refuge's visitor center opened in 1994, the refuge itself was established by Franklin Delano Roosevelt in 1936 and at that time was the first and only unit of the National Wildlife Refuge system devoted to research. With an inquisitive child and a set of binoculars, you can undertake some research of your own here.

EATS FOR KIDS Although picnicking is not allowed, on a pleasant day you may bring snacks to eat on the Visitor Center patio. Otherwise, the staff at the front desk can direct you to local fast-food restaurants, many of which are along Route 197. A 15-minute drive away in Laurel, **Pasta Plus** (209 Gorman Ave., tel. 301/498–5100) serves up homemade pastas, breads, and desserts, which you can also carry out.

PHILLIPS COLLECTION

If you arrive by Metro, check out the Phillips Collection's poster at the Dupont Circle station. It's a good appetite whetter for this kid-comfortable museum, where you can sit back on a puffy couch or plop down on the carpet. In a former home—albeit a grand one—artworks are arranged in 25 galleries, 10 of which are the size of bedrooms. Six fireplaces and one fake fireplace (which looks real) add to the museum's homey feel. Unlike most other galleries, where uniformed guards appear uninterested in the masterpieces around them, the Phillips employs art students, many of whom are artists themselves, to sit by the paintings and answer questions.

The collection's best-known painting, Pierre-Auguste Renoir's *Luncheon of the Boating Party*, is particularly interesting to children because of its bright colors, the people engaged in happy conversation, and the terrier on the table. Other paintings that kids can relate to depict a ballet rehearsal, by Edgar Degas; a bullfight, by Pablo Picasso; and children playing hide-and-seek in a 19th-century house, by William Merritt Chase. Works by Swiss painter

KEEP IN MIND During the gallery's popular Family Free Days, held annually the first weekend in June, you can take part in projects (on a walk-in basis) that could entail anything from creative collage making to key-chain making to live music. Throughout the year, hands-on workshops for children and their parents ($10–$15 per adult-child pair) revolve around special exhibits and themes. Kids might find themselves at a photo shoot or making sculpture.

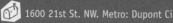
1600 21st St. NW. Metro: Dupont Circle

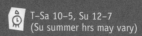
T–Sa 10–5, Su 12–7
(Su summer hrs may vary)

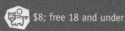
$8; free 18 and under

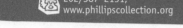
202/387–2151;
www.phillipscollection.org

5 and up, workshops
6 and up

Paul Klee also appeal to kids. His little paintings look as though they employ hieroglyphic symbols.

Gather a group of five or more kids (and call four weeks in advance) for a personal tour arranged around the theme of Art of the City. The tour includes interactive activities led by the museum's enthusiastic education staff. If you don't have time to book an advance tour or if the idea of being with more than a couple of kids seems daunting, you can call ahead for a family fun pack (and impress your kids with your knowledge) or pick one up at the museum's entrance. Each pack includes artwork to discover, postcards or pictures, and activities you can try at home so the fun continues long after you've left.

HEY, KIDS! The Phillips Collection staff requests that everyone keep a safe distance—12 inches—from all paintings and sculpture, because artwork can be damaged by accident.

EATS FOR KIDS There are plenty of quick and inexpensive places to eat around Dupont Circle. For pizza, gyros, and other Greek concoctions made with tomato and cheese, try **Zorba's Café** (1612 20th St. NW, tel. 202/387–8555). At Kramers Books and Afterwards Café (1517 Connecticut Ave., NW, tel. 202/387–3825), you can buy a book and enjoy it with breakfast, lunch, or dinner.

ROCK CREEK PARK

The biggest stretch of parkland in Washington, Rock Creek Park offers a wealth of activities.

Take a walk *in* the wild side at the nature center, which brings the outdoors in. Pelts, bones, feathers, and a bird's nest occupy a touch table in the lobby, while another room contains stuffed animals representative of mid-Atlantic fauna. Preschoolers put on puppet shows featuring their forest friends in the Discovery Room. Downstairs, elementary schoolchildren use mice (the computer kind) to discover even more about the park's ecosystem. A 75-seat planetarium introduces youngsters to the solar system, and some shows include a Native American legend about a coyote who threw rocks to make pictures in the sky.

Take a hike on any of several trails near the center, but first pick up a discovery pack for each child at the front desk. Packs are equipped with binoculars, a field microscope, and a magnifying lens. The 15- to 20-minute Edge of the Woods trail, a flat, asphalt loop

HEY, KIDS!

If you're 6–12, ask for a Junior Ranger activity book. When you complete at least five of the eight activities, show the book to a ranger. You'll get a signed certificate and a Junior Ranger patch with a pair of raccoons on it. Display it with pride.

KEEP IN MIND

The planetarium offers free weekend shows at 1 for ages 4 and up (also on Wednesday at 4) and at 4 for ages 7 and up. Children under the recommended ages may find the shows either boring or scary. (Before shows, the sun is shown setting over the Washington skyline; at the end, it rises and the room brightens.) If you skip the shows, you can still light up the sky by turning off the lights in the Discovery Room; glow-in-the-dark stickers cover the ceiling.

5200 Glover Rd. NW; stables 5100 Glover Rd. NW (between 16th St. and Connecticut Ave., south of Military Rd.)

 202/895–6070 nature center, 202/362–0117 stables; www.nps.gov/rocr/

 Free; pony rides $20 for 15 min; trail rides $30 per hr

 Daily sunrise–sunset; nature center W–Su 9–5; pony rides Sa–Su 12–3; trail rides T–Th 3, Sa–Su 12, 1:30, and 3

 2 and up, pony rides 4–7 (min 30"), trail rides 12 and up

perfect for preschoolers and strollers, goes to a pond a little larger than a bathtub, where tadpoles swim in spring. For older children, the Woodland Trail takes 40–60 minutes, depending on how often you stop to search for animals crawling on the forest floor or chirping atop the trees. On most weekends at 2, rangers lead hikes on topics ranging from the lowly worm to the majestic wolf.

Take to the saddle: Rock Creek is the only place in town where kids can become urban cowboys and cowgirls (closed-toe shoes, preferably with a small heel, are required). Pony rides (reservations required) aren't just a trip around a circle; they're 15-minute rides through the woods. Many preschoolers aren't ready for this excursion, but kids over 8 might find it babyish, since a teenage guide holds the reins. Before and after, kids are encouraged to pat their pony. On 1-hour trail rides, guides take groups along some of the same wooded trails that Presidents Martin Van Buren, Teddy Roosevelt, and Ronald Reagan and World War II general George Patton once rode.

EATS FOR KIDS Picnic areas are near the nature center. Pack a lunch from **Magruder's Grocery Store** (3627 Connecticut Ave. NW, tel. 202/237–2531), a 5- to 10-minute drive from the nature center. Near Magruder's are two inexpensive restaurants: **American City Diner** (5532 Connecticut Ave. NW, tel. 202/244–1949) and **Bread and Chocolate** (5542 Connecticut Ave. NW, tel. 202/966–7413), for those who want a more healthful meal with an elegant dessert. If your child doesn't care for éclairs or other pastries, don't worry; cookies are available, too.

ROOSEVELT ISLAND

If the wildest animal your children ever want to see is a computer mouse, Roosevelt Island isn't for your family. But for kids who believe, as Theodore Roosevelt did, that "There is delight in the hardy life of the open," this sanctuary is a superb place to get away from the city's concrete, crowds, and cars. If it weren't for the airplanes from Ronald Reagan National Airport roaring overhead, you might forget you were in D.C. altogether.

Leave your car in the parking lot next to the George Washington Memorial Parkway and walk over the bridge to this island wilderness preserve in the Potomac River. The 90-acre tribute to the conservation-minded 26th president includes 2½ miles of nature trails that crisscross marshland, swampland, and upland forest.

In the center of the island is a clearing, where a 17-foot bronze statue of Roosevelt stands, his right hand raised for emphasis. He is surrounded by shallow pools, fountains, and four large stone tablets inscribed with his thoughts on nature, manhood, state (government),

KEEP IN MIND After you cross the bridge, you'll see a large bulletin board where you can pick up a trail guide. Encourage your children to stay on the marked trails. Off the trails you may encounter poison ivy and great nettles, a 3-foot-tall plant better known as stinging nettles because you'll feel a stinging pain if you rub against it. Gather a group of 10 or more people and call a week in advance for a guided tour led by a park ranger, who will point out a lot more than where the stinging nettles are.

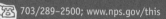

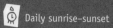

and youth. For example, he advised students at the Groton School in Massachusetts, "Keep your eyes on the stars, but remember to keep your feet on the ground." And there is plenty of ground for your feet to cover at Roosevelt Island.

To make the most of your visit, pack a backpack with some of the following items for your children: binoculars, a magnifying glass, a sketch pad and crayons or markers, a camera, and plant and animal guidebooks, if you have them. Cattails, arrow arum, pickerelweed, willow, ash, maple, and oak all grow on the island, which is also a habitat for frogs, raccoons, birds, squirrels, and the occasional red or gray fox. But you won't see the animal most people associate with Roosevelt: the teddy bear.

HEY, KIDS! How did the Rough Rider known for carrying "a big stick" inspire a stuffed animal? Once, when Roosevelt was hunting, his aides tied up an old bear for him to kill. But he couldn't shoot the defenseless animal, prompting a toy maker to create the teddy bear.

EATS FOR KIDS There's nothing to buy on this island—not even a soda. You may not want to drink too much anyway, since public rest rooms close between mid-November and early April. If you're coming from D.C., consider a stop in Georgetown first. You can pick up sandwiches, fried chicken, and salads at **Safeway** (1855 Wisconsin Ave. NW, tel. 202/333-3223). Then bring a blanket to the island, spread out near the statue, and listen to the music of birds as you eat.

Imagine your children making an animal paperweight or sketching on a scroll while learning about ancient art techniques, geography, or other cultures. It's all part of the Freer and Sackler Galleries' ImaginAsia program. Armed with guidebook and pencil, children (and their parents) search for ceramics, sculpture, and paintings and then go beyond simply writing about what they see. They may locate on a map where a work or an artist is from, interpret works, describe how they feel, or even invent stories. Afterward, you all meet in an education room, where your kids can create a take-home craft related to the exhibits seen. The program is operated on a drop-in basis; reservations are only required for groups of eight or more.

Even if you're not visiting on a program day, there's plenty here to interest your kids. Activity-filled guidebooks are available at each museum's information desk. And just why are there two museums, you might be wondering.

KEEP IN MIND Guidebooks list activities for a broad range of ages and abilities. Parents of young children will need to work with their kids to decide what's appropriate. Most children 10 and up can probably decide for themselves which activities are suitable.

HEY, KIDS! While you're in the Peacock Room, think about the real peacocks that used to live at the gallery. In 1993, a peacock named James and a peahen named Sylvia resided in the museum's courtyard. After one year, the gallery needed to find a new home for the birds because Sylvia laid too many eggs. James and Sylvia lived with a farmer who loved them because they squawked to alert her when visitors arrived.

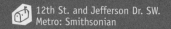 12th St. and Jefferson Dr. SW.
Metro: Smithsonian

 Free

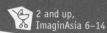 Daily 10–5:30

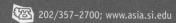 202/357-2700; www.asia.si.edu

2 and up,
ImaginAsia 6–14

The Freer Gallery, which contains one of the world's finest collections of Asian masterpieces, was endowed by Charles Freer, who insisted on a few conditions: Objects in the collection could not be loaned out, nor could objects from outside the collection be put on display. Because of the latter, the connected Sackler Gallery was built. Like the Freer, the Sackler focuses on works from throughout Asia, but it also mounts visiting exhibits. The Freer's exhibits do change, however, but only because its permanent collection is so massive.

The Freer's collection also includes works by American artists influenced by the Orient. One such was Freer's friend James McNeill Whistler, who introduced him to Asian art. On display in Gallery 12 is Whistler's Peacock Room, a blue-and-gold painted dining room, decorated with painted leather, wood, and canvas and, as the name implies, devoted to peacocks. Freer paid $42,000 for the entire room and moved it from London to the United States in 1904. Perhaps your children will be influenced by the Asian masterpieces they see or inspired to decorate their bedrooms with a particular theme.

EATS FOR KIDS For restaurant choices, *see* any of the listings for museums on the Mall: the Castle, Hirshhorn Museum and Sculpture Garden (summer only), National Air and Space Museum, National Gallery of Art and Sculpture Garden, National Museum of American History, and National Museum of Natural History.

SIX FLAGS AMERICA

ashington is known for its educational and economical attractions. Six Flags America, the capital area's only theme park, isn't one of them. What it is, however, is exciting. Actually a combination theme park and water park (dubbed Paradise Island), it contains more than 100 rides, shows, and games spread over 150 acres in suburban Prince George's County.

On the "dry" side, roller coaster revelers have eight fast choices. The Wild One is a more-than-80-year-old classic wooden coaster. Roar mixes old-fashioned wood and modern computer technology to produce a thrilling ride. The five steel coasters are Batwing, Superman–Ride of Steel, the Mind Eraser, the Joker's Jinx, and Two-Face: The Flip Side, which takes you through a 72-foot-high vertical loop—twice. Coaster traditionalists prefer the jiggle and clackety-clack sounds of the "woodie." Metal coasters follow a more circuitous route, with corkscrew turns and 360° loops. If your youngsters aren't tall enough (all rides, including the coasters, have height restrictions), head to Looney Tunes Movie Town, where even toddlers

HEY, KIDS! It takes about a million gallons to fill up the Monsoon Lagoon—enough to fill 16,666 bathtubs. Approximately 10,000 pounds of sugar are used to make the roughly 100,000 servings of candy sold here each year—the same amount you'd use if you felt like baking nearly 1½ million chocolate chip cookies. As for hot dogs, if lined up tip to tip, the approximately 188,000 half-foot-longs sold annually would stretch the length of the Mall—about nine times.

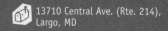 13710 Central Ave. (Rte. 214), Largo, MD

 301/249–1500; www.sixflags.com

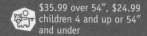 $35.99 over 54", $24.99 children 4 and up or 54" and under

 Mid-Apr–May, Sa–Su 10:30–6; Memorial Day–mid-June, M–F 10–6, Sa–Su 10:30–9; mid-June–Labor Day, daily 10:30–9

 2 and up

can coast on a mini-coaster, get behind the wheel of pint-size 18-wheeler, or earn their wings by flying minijets.

On the "wet" side, kids like Crocodile Cal's Outback Beach House. Water-powered activities here include a barrel that dumps 1,000 gallons of water on unsuspecting passers-by every few minutes. The Monsoon Lagoon wave pool has a graduated entrance so even water babies (with parents, of course) can splash around.

Naturally everyone needs to pack swimsuits, sunscreen, and sunglasses for a fun-filled day at this entertainment complex, but parents should also bring lots of money and patience. Especially on weekends, lines begin forming even before the park opens. Most families end up spending about six to eight hours here, made easier by the availability of stroller and locker rentals. So you won't learn about American history or government. You'll still have a blast.

EATS FOR KIDS
No outside food is permitted, though you can bring in one sealed bottle of water per person. Vendors provide complimentary cups of water and ice. Inside, you'll find funnel cakes and cotton candy, hot dogs, buffalo wings, and ice cream. The **Hollywood Backlot Café**, **Heritage House,** and **Crazy Horse Saloon** are air-conditioned.

KEEP IN MIND To maximize your chances of minimizing expenses and aggravation, prepare ahead. Look for discount coupons at grocery stores, or consider a season pass, which includes discounts at other Six Flags parks. If your child (or your arms) needs a stroller, bring your own to save the rental fee. Discuss spending limits with your kids beforehand, not after they see things they must have. To avoid crowds, go on Monday or Tuesday, and make a plan upon arrival, doing what most interests your kids early. Time flies when you're having fun.

SULLY HISTORIC SITE

As at other local historic sites, kids can get a real feel for how people lived two centuries ago at this museum dedicated to life in the Federal Period (1790–1820). Your children may pretend to wash dishes in an old stone sink, cool off with a folded fan, or use sugar nippers. They may soak up the scent of the green and black teas that were popular at the time or get a whiff of No. 7, a cologne that George Washington (and more recently John F. Kennedy) wore. But kids also learn that life wasn't so sweet then, and not just because the early 1800s lacked our modern amenities. Slavery, too, is addressed, and your children can handle replicas of the passes that slaves needed to leave the property or lift the heavy cast ironware used in the kitchen.

Sully was the understated 1794 country home of Richard Bland Lee, uncle of Confederate general Robert E. Lee; his wife, Elizabeth Collins Lee; and their children. As Virginia's first representative to Congress, Lee cast one of two swing votes that put the nation's capital in his backyard.

KEEP IN MIND Some of the stairs in the Sully mansion are steep, so make sure unsteady toddlers, unsteady grandparents, and distracted parents are extra careful. Strollers are not permitted in the house.

HEY, KIDS! As you look at the picture of the Lee family crest in the house, notice the squirrel on it. When the Lee children were living here, they had a pet white squirrel. One day the squirrel was let loose in the house. Imagine the excitement as the kids tried to keep their little pet from escaping outside. Can you spot the stuffed white squirrel in the parlor?

 3601 Sully Rd., Chantilly, VA

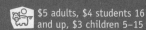 $5 adults, $4 students 16 and up, $3 children 5–15

 W–M 11–4

703/437–1794; www.co.fairfax.va.us/parks

 5 and up

Purchase tickets and even souvenirs in a one-room, log schoolhouse that was used in nearby Haymarket during the early to mid-19th century. In this tiny room, about a half-dozen children studied under a teacher who lived above the classroom.

Guides, often Fairfax County Park Authority volunteers, conduct 1-hour tours of the Lee house on the hour. Upon request, they may tailor their talk to your family's special interests (textiles or cooking, for example) and show you the outbuildings and gardens. Weather permitting, there is also a regular tour of the outbuildings, including reconstructed slave quarters, at 2. Most spring and summer weekends are especially festive, with such special events as soap making, quilting, bread baking, candle making, and children's games.

After touring Sully, you may take advantage of its 127 acres. Watch as airplanes zip by or watch your own kids zip by as they run and jump on ground where children played centuries ago.

UNITED STATES BOTANIC GARDEN

F ollow your nose. Or your eyes. Or your sense of humor. Or just follow the meandering paths around the amazing conservatory here. It's full of gardens to delight the senses and tickle the fancy with exotic, strange, rare, and beautiful plants from all over the world.

George Washington, Thomas Jefferson, and James Madison imagined a national botanic garden. Congress established the garden in 1820, the first greenhouse opened in 1842, and the conservatory was completed in 1933. Recently, this national treasure underwent a renovation: Gardeners sifted through thousands of plants and tons of dirt during the 4-year, $34 million restoration, and a conservatory wilder than the founding fathers could have imagined reopened in 2001, to the delight of botany lovers big and small.

Kids can see plants that dinosaurs might have munched on at the Garden Primeval. Look down at the pathway for footprints from baby and grownup dinosaurs. To learn how plants grow up to become today's products, from fragrances to food, head to the Garden Court.

HEY, KIDS! You've heard of space explorers and sea explorers. Did you know there are plant explorers? You can become one, too. Find the tree named for George Washington. Then find the "Teddy bear" tree in the Jungle. In the Canopy Walk, see how many different epiphytes you can find. These plants don't require soil to grow.

100 Maryland Ave. SW.
Metro: Federal Center Southwest

 Free

 Daily 10–5

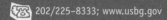 202/225-8333; www.usbg.gov

 2 and up

See how bananas grow upside down from 20-foot stalks. Then check out the therapeutic uses of the specimens in Medicinal Plants.

Ironically, the Meditation Garden is full of plants with funny names, such as devil's shoestring, sticky monkey flower, and bushy skullcap. In the World Desert, cacti grow sharp spines (some of which look like fishhooks) as protection from grazing animals, though of course they aren't in any danger here. A sign explains how cacti expand and contract like accordions.

Children may not be enchanted until they discover more about this diverse flowering family. For example, the Beard Orchid looks like it sprouted whiskers, and the Mirror Orchid attracts male wasps because its flowers look like female wasps. See what's in bloom when you visit, and allow at least an hour—enough time to plant some seeds of wisdom in your own little gardeners.

EATS FOR KIDS
Though orchids hardly look appetizing, some kinds of vanilla ice cream contain flavoring from the cured seedpod of an orchid called *Vanilla planifolia*. For ice cream and other foods, check out the eateries under the United States Capitol, the National Gallery of Art, and the National Air and Space Museum.

KEEP IN MIND Read the signs carefully. Kids should not touch plants unless the staff invites them to feel a particular one. Just as at other museums, children should be encouraged to walk and use indoor voices as they explore. Though the conservatory is wheelchair accessible, if you're pushing a double stroller, you'll find the kind that puts children one in front of the other works best here.

UNITED STATES CAPITOL

Throughout the Capitol, statues, paintings, and even rooms reveal much about the people and events that shaped our nation. The frieze around the rim of the Rotunda depicts 400 years of recognizable American history. Columbus's arrival, the California Gold Rush, and the Wright brothers' historic flight are all here. Eight immense oil paintings depict historical scenes, four from the Revolutionary War period. See if your child can find Pocahontas in the Rotunda. (*Hint*: She's in three places and she doesn't resemble Disney's cartoon.)

South of the Rotunda is Statuary Hall. Here and throughout the building are statues representing each state, which your kids can search for. They range from Colorado's (and *Apollo 13*'s) Jack Swigert to Utah's Philo Farnsworth, the father of TV. Capitol guides (wearing bright red) can help you locate statues.

On the north (Senate) side, you can look into the chamber once used by the Supreme Court where the Dred Scott case was argued and the movie *Armistad* was filmed. In

EATS FOR KIDS A public **dining room** (tel. 202/224–4870), open for lunch M–F, Senate-side, has served Senate bean soup, a favorite with legislators, every day since 1901. The **Longworth Cafeteria** (tel. 202/225–0878), on the House side, offers Mexican, Italian, and deli food.

HEY, KIDS! Except for 1814–1819, when it was closed after the British burned part of the Capitol during the War of 1812, Statuary Hall was home to the House of Representatives 1807–1857. Because of its perfectly elliptical ceiling, strange things happen to sound. A slight whisper spoken on one side of the hall could—and still can—be heard on the other. On tour, try it. If the room isn't too noisy, the trick may work.

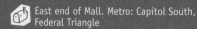 East end of Mall. Metro: Capitol South, Federal Triangle

202/224–3121, 202/225–6827 recording, 202/224–3235 guide service; www.aoc.gov

Free, timed-entry passes given out beginning at 9 AM at the kiosk at 1st St. and Independence Ave.

M–Sa 9–4; hrs subject to change

7 and up

the ground-floor Brumidi Corridor, frescoes and oil paintings of birds, plants, American inventions, and even the *Challenger* crew adorn the walls.

For a chance to observe Congress in action, visit your congressperson's office and ask what services they provide. You may get a free gallery pass or even the chance to hop the miniature subway in the basement to the House and Senate office buildings.

As beautiful as the building is, so are the grounds, landscaped in the late-19th century by Frederick Law Olmsted. On these 68 acres you'll find the city's tamest squirrels (don't get too close; they might bite), a waterfall, and many TV news correspondents, all jockeying for position in front of the Capitol for their "stand-ups." Encourage your kids to look up at the Capitol dome. The figure on top, which some might mistake for another Pocahontas, is Freedom.

KEEP IN MIND To take the 30-minute guided tour, plan for at least another 30 minutes of waiting and going through security. To enhance your children's appreciation, talk about Congress's role in our government and the Capitol's place in history before you arrive. Then during the tour, encourage them to move up front to see and hear better. Sometimes kids want to know how long it took to build the Capitol. The answer: 200 years and still building.

UNITED STATES HOLOCAUST
MEMORIAL MUSEUM

Like the history it covers, the Holocaust Museum can be profoundly disturbing, so you should first decide whether your children can appreciate it. The recommended ages published by the museum are guidelines only. The subject matter is complex. The museum is often crowded, making it difficult to see. The average visit is long, often 2–3 hours, and exhibits involve lots of reading. All that said, a trip here will be memorable for a preteen or teenager.

The museum tells the story of the 11 million Jews, Gypsies, Poles, Jehovah's Witnesses, homosexuals, political prisoners, and others killed by the Nazis between 1933 and 1945. Striving to give a you-are-there experience, the graphic presentation is as extraordinary as the subject matter: Upon arrival, each visitor is issued an "identity card" containing biographical information on a real person from the Holocaust. As you move through the museum, you read sequential updates on your card. The museum recounts the Holocaust through documentary films, videotaped and audiotaped oral histories, and a collection that includes such items as a chilling freight car, like those used to transport Jews from Warsaw

KEEP IN MIND You will need a same-day, timed-entry pass to get into the permanent exhibition, or you can call www.tickets.com for advance passes (fee charged). Ideally, it might be best for you to visit the museum without your children first to determine if it's appropriate. If that's not possible, consider going through Daniel's Story first. Even for teenagers, Daniel's Story will be meaningful, and you can then gauge whether to proceed.

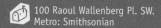
100 Raoul Wallenberg Pl. SW.
Metro: Smithsonian

202/488-0400, 800/400-9373
ProTix; www.ushmm.org

Free; advance passes
through www.tickets.com $1.75
each plus $1 per order

Daily 10–5:30; early Apr–mid-June,
T and Th 'til 8

11 and up, Remember the
Children 8 and up

to the Treblinka death camp. Although there are four privacy walls to protect visitors from especially graphic images, they don't cover all that is horrific. After this powerful experience, the adjacent Hall of Remembrance provides space for quiet reflection. If your children have further questions, take advantage of the computers in the Wexner Learning Center.

You don't need a pass for Remember the Children: Daniel's Story, an exhibit that follows one family. Children know from the beginning that Daniel survives to share his story. In this interactive exhibit, your children can follow events in Daniel's life. For example, they can see and touch the cookies in his well-stocked 1933 kitchen, but can only look at the one turnip in a pot on the stove of his 1944 ghetto apartment. At the end of the exhibit, kids are invited to write about their thoughts and feelings. It's a helpful outlet after this moving experience.

EATS FOR KIDS
The museum's **café**, open 8:30–4:30, offers a variety of dishes, including matzoh-ball soup and potato knishes, kosher Asian noodle salads, and even peanut butter and jelly sandwiches.

HEY, KIDS! The doll on the second floor was made especially for a Polish Jewish girl named Zofia Burowska. Zofia kept the doll, even when she was in the Kraków ghetto, but when she was deported out of the ghetto, she gave the doll to a non-Jewish family, who saved it for her. Zofia survived, and after the war she and the doll were reunited.

UNITED STATES NATIONAL ARBORETUM

How does your garden grow? Here the garden grows with priceless, 350-year-old trees smaller than a 2-year-old, herbs, an aquatic garden, and 15,000 magnificent azaleas. The arboretum has two entrances: New York Avenue and R Street, off Bladensburg Road. Whichever you choose, your first stop should be the administration building, where you'll see speckled, bright orange koi flourishing in the surrounding pool. Some are as long as a child's arm, others as little as a finger. (Feed the fish for a quarter. Look for machines that look like they would contain gumballs.) Pick up a map inside. You'll need it. Almost 10 miles of winding roads cover 446 acres of botanical masterpieces.

Make sure you visit the National Bonsai and Penjing Museum. (In Japan artistic potted plants are bonsai and in China tray landscapes are called *penjing*.) These arts have been depicted in Chinese paintings as early as the 6th century. The idea is simple: Just as you get your hair cut to achieve a desired look, so these trees are trimmed for a desired look, which varies by species. The trees are worth, "about as much as your children," according

EATS FOR KIDS You're not allowed to pick the fruits, vegetables, or herbs, no matter how tempting they appear. (Think the Garden of Eden.) But you can enjoy typical vendor fare such as hot dogs, nachos, and ice cream bars from mid-April to mid-October at the **Arboretum Café.** Or you can bring your own and take advantage of picnic tables under the state trees.

 3501 New York Ave. NE

 Free; tram $4 adults, $2 children 4–16

202/245–2726;
www.USNA.usda.gov

Daily 8–5; National
Penjing Museum daily

2 and up

to the curator. Many have been nurtured for generations, and some were gifts to presidents. Your children might enjoy wandering through outdoor rooms in search of the oldest trees, the smallest trees, or those with interesting trunks.

Follow your nose to the National Herb Garden, where herbs from around the world are arranged. Experience aloe, oregano, wild strawberries, licorice, English lavender, and ginger. Hundreds of heritage roses also bloom here. Fruits, vegetables, and flowers thrive in the Youth Garden, planted by schoolkids, who share what they grow with the homeless.

But plants aren't the only things jutting out from the earth. Twenty-two sandstone Corinthian columns that once stood at the east portico of the U.S. Capitol are set in a rectangle in a meadow. Within them is a fountain, where water flows into a reflecting pool.

HEY, KIDS! Do you know your state tree? At the National Grove of State Trees, you can search for the official trees of all 50 states and the District of Columbia. Pick up a state tree list at the administration building. Don't look for markers on the ground; identification tags hang from the branches.

KEEP IN MIND You may drive, bike, walk, or do a little of each around the arboretum. Walking is pleasant, especially with a stroller, but you can't cover much ground. You'll get farther biking, and racks for locking your bicycle are scattered about the collection. Driving is slow—the speed limit is 20 mph and enforced—but you can park at each garden/museum within the arboretum and then walk around. On weekends mid-April–mid-October, there's a 40-minute narrated tram ride that older children may enjoy.

e prepared for your kids to ask some serious questions about war and death after visiting this moving memorial to the 58,235 men and women who died in Vietnam. Sometimes children think they're all buried at the monument. They aren't, of course, but the slabs of black granite inscribed with the names of the dead are as somber, as powerful, and as evocative of poignant reflection as any cemetery.

Known as "the Wall," the memorial is one of the most visited sites in Washington. Conceived by Jan Scruggs, a former infantry corporal who had served in Vietnam, these black granite panels that reflect the sky, the trees, and the faces of those looking for names (and perhaps crying when they find them) was designed by Maya Ying Lin, a 21-year-old architectural student at Yale. The nontraditional war memorial was originally decried by some veterans, but with the addition of a flagpole just south of the Wall as well as Frederick Hart's statue of three soldiers, most critics were won over. When one young boy saw the statue for the first time, he exclaimed, "Look mom. They're just boys."

EATS FOR KIDS Grab a hot dog or hamburger at a **food kiosk** behind the nearby Korean War Veterans Memorial.

HEY, KIDS! You and your parents may be surprised to hear that although 10,000 women served in Vietnam, only eight women's names are on the Wall. One of these is Mary Klinker, a nurse involved in Operation Baby Lift, a mission to bring Vietnamese orphans to the United States. Klinker's plane crashed in 1975. As a memorial to these women, a stirring sculpture depicts two uniformed women caring for a wounded male soldier while a third woman kneels nearby.

Constitution Gardens, 22nd St. and Constitution Ave. NW. Metro: Foggy Bottom

 Free

24 hrs; staffed daily 8 AM–midnight

 202/426–6841; www.nps.gov/vive

 9 and up

People's names appear on the Wall in the order of the date they died. To look up a name yourself, refer to the books posted at the entrance and exit of the memorial. Children may make rubbings of names at the memorial. For help, see a park ranger.

One of the most stirring aspects of the memorial are all the flowers and mementos left in remembrance, and your child may wonder what becomes of all of them. A small selection, including wedding rings, a baseball, letters, and photographs are on display on the third floor of the National Museum of American History (see #27). Other items are stored in a warehouse in Landover, Maryland, where they are fast becoming another memorial.

KEEP IN MIND Visiting the Wall might well be one of your children's most meaningful experiences in Washington, especially if you have any memories of the war or the times that you are willing to share. Giving your personal perspective, even if limited, can bring the memorial alive in a way that a drier, more historical discussion can't. Help is available from rangers when your kids have questions that you can't answer.

WASHINGTON DOLLS' HOUSE & TOY MUSEUM

6

Some people say it's the little things in life that have the most meaning. At this quaint museum, children learn about the past from the little things that mean the most to them: dolls, toys, and games. Since this is a serious collection for doll enthusiasts, most displays are behind glass, preventing you from having to repeat, "Don't touch."

Tucked away behind Wisconsin Avenue's shopping malls, this small, yellow-brick house with a flag in front is an unexpected place for a museum celebrating the past. Purchase tickets in the front lobby at an old post office window surrounded by miniature toys in mail slots. Dollhouses are arranged in six small galleries—in some rooms from floor to ceiling—and cats lurk in almost every structure. But there's more to this museum than traditional dollhouses. Shops; stables; a one-room schoolhouse; a turn-of-the-20th-century quintet of Baltimore row houses; a 1903 New Jersey seaside hotel; and an elaborate Mexican house with an aviary, a working elevator, and a garage with a vintage automobile help youngsters appreciate how people lived in different places and at different times.

EATS FOR KIDS A block up Jenifer Street from the museum is **Booeymonger** (5252A Wisconsin Ave. NW, tel. 202/686–5805), known for creative sandwiches. For the usual fare, go to **McDonald's** (5300 Wisconsin Ave. NW, tel. 202/244–1122), on the lower level of the nearby Mazza Gallerie. Or cross Wisconsin Avenue and join the line at the **Corner Bakery** (5333 Wisconsin Ave. NW, tel. 202/237–2200), where your children can look through the glass to see what they want to eat before they order. Each children's meal comes with a drink and a choice of cookie (oatmeal raisin, sugar, peanut butter, or classic chocolate chip).

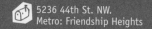
5236 44th St. NW.
Metro: Friendship Heights

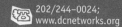
202/244-0024;
www.dcnetworks.org

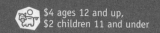
$4 ages 12 and up,
$2 children 11 and under

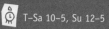
T–Sa 10–5, Su 12–5

4 and up

Antique toys and games include an Old Maid card game, circus performers and animals, dominoes the size of a child's fingernails, and many tea sets. Noah's arks and animals are examples of "Sunday toys," which children could only play with on Sundays in some religious families. Imagine keeping Sunday's toys separate from Monday's these days!

Pastimes such as baseball and holidays are observed with special exhibits. Come at Christmas and you'll see a revolving musical tree. During February, you'll see Victorian valentines. You can even celebrate your child's birthday with a party in the museum's Edwardian tea room. (George W. Bush's twins celebrated their birthday here when their grandfather was president.)

One museum shop is dedicated to dollhouse furniture and accessories for collectors; the other carries kid-friendly merchandise.

HEY, KIDS! Have you ever tried to make a house out of paper? It's harder than it looks. In 1884, when Gertrude Horsey Smith (yes, that was her middle name) was about 12, she made a paper house. You can see this house in the lobby of the museum. Be sure to turn the table around to see the back of the house, so you can look at the paper piano, dining room set, and more.

KEEP IN MIND
If your child gets bored and needs a little action, you can ask a museum staffer to send a 1930s Lionel train whizzing and whistling around its tracks. Kids can also pull a string to ring the bell at an old Ohio schoolhouse.

WASHINGTON MONUMENT

Some kids say the Washington Monument looks like a giant pencil. Others think this 555'5" obelisk (10 times as tall as its width at the base) punctuates the capital like a huge, partially buried exclamation point. Visible from nearly everywhere in the city, it's a landmark for visiting tourists and lost motorists alike and a beacon for anyone who yearns to shoot to the top and survey all of Washington below.

A limited number of free tickets, good for a half-hour period, are available at the kiosk on 15th Street beginning at 8 AM. Advance tickets are available from reservations.nps.gov. Arrive at the monument at the appointed time. Although lines to get in may be long, they move quickly. If your children are restless, have them count the flags surrounding the monument. (There are 50: one for each state, though none for the District of Columbia.) Once you're inside, an elevator whizzes to the top in just 70 seconds, a trip that originally took about 12 minutes in a steam-powered elevator back in 1888 when the monument opened to visitors. Here you can enjoy a bird's-eye view of the city for as long as you like.

EATS FOR KIDS

A refreshment stand at the bottom of the hill sells ice cream in summer and hot chocolate in winter, as well as sandwiches. For some down-to-earth good food, *see* the restaurants listed for the United States Holocaust Memorial Museum and National Museum of American History.

HEY, KIDS!

It took more than 50 years to build this monument. Fund-raising began in 1833, and the cornerstone was laid in 1848. However, by 1854, construction had stopped because the Washington National Monument Society ran out of funds. (Look for a ring about a third of the way up; the marble used to complete the monument later was of a slightly different shade.) Cattle roamed around and Union troops were trained here. After the Civil War, Congress helped fund the monument and in 1884, the monument was finally completed, becoming the world's tallest structure.

15th St. and Constitution Ave. NW.
Metro: Smithsonian

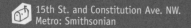 202/426-6841, 800/967-2283 advance
tickets; www.nps.gov/wamo

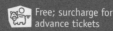 Free; surcharge for
advance tickets

 Daily 9–5

 5 and up

Each of the four sides has two viewing stations, and every other station is equipped with a step. Small children may think Washington looks like Legoland. Older children may enjoy trying to find Washington's landmarks. (A street map, available in the gift shop, is helpful for this.) On a very clear day, you can see Shenandoah National Park to the west and the stadium where the Washington Redskins play to the east.

When you're ready to land, descend one flight of stairs to the elevator. This level also houses a small bookshop that carries a modest selection of children's books about Washington the place and Washington the man. Then circle the flags surrounding the building, and take a good look at the top of the monument. Unlike a pencil lead (made of graphite), the monument is topped with a 7½-pound piece of aluminum, a very expensive metal in 1884, when the monument was completed.

KEEP IN MIND Judging by the crowds, it seems there are as many people who want to look down on the Washington action literally as there are those who look down on it figuratively. If you don't want to wait in line, head to Washington National Cathedral's Pilgrim Observation Gallery (see #4), which offers an awesome view, too.

WASHINGTON NATIONAL CATHEDRAL

4

Boys and girls go Gothic at this, the sixth-largest cathedral in the world. Like its 14th-century counterparts, the National Cathedral (officially Washington's Cathedral Church of St. Peter and St. Paul) has a nave, flying buttresses, and vaults that were built stone by stone. Fanciful gargoyles adorn the outside of the building. Inside, a stained-glass window with an encapsulated moon rock celebrates the *Apollo 11* space flight, and statues of George Washington and Abraham Lincoln stand as tributes. Pick up a children's guide to the cathedral at the front door or at the Medieval Workshop in the cathedral's crypt.

Aside from seeing the cathedral itself, however, there are lots of other activities for kids. At Medieval Workshops (Sa 10–2), your children can create a clay gargoyle, carve limestone, piece together a stained-glass window, and make a brass rubbing while learning about life in the Middle Ages. You can drop in but workshops are not drop-off affairs: those under 12 must be accompanied by an adult. Keep in mind that if you're also with children younger than 5 there's little in the crypt to entertain them.

EATS FOR KIDS The only place to get something to eat on the cathedral grounds is the **museum shop** (tel. 202/537–6267), which has sandwiches and yogurt in a self-serve refrigerator. The cathedral is surrounded by green gardens that are great for a picnic, however. A few blocks north you'll find **Cactus Cantina** (3300 Wisconsin Ave. NW, tel. 202/686–7222), a lively Mexican restaurant, and **Cafe Deluxe** (3228 Wisconsin Ave. NW, tel. 202/686–2233), which includes a three-vegetable entrée among its children's offerings.

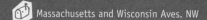 Massachusetts and Wisconsin Aves. NW

 202/537-6200, 202/537-2934 Medieval Workshops; www.cathedral.org

 Free; most children's programs $6

 Memorial Day–Labor Day, M–F 10–9, Sa–Su 10–4:30; early Sept–late May, daily 10–4:30

4 and up, Medieval Workshops 5 and up

On Family Saturdays, children 4–8 explore the nooks and crannies of the cathedral before making such crafts as dyed Easter eggs, arranging fresh flowers, making gingerbread cathedrals, and creating mosaics with glass tiles.

Also of interest to young and old, the Pilgrim Observation Gallery provides a panoramic view of Washington. A charming children's chapel with kneelers depicts the story of Noah's ark, a maze is outside in the Bishop's Garden, and a greenhouse contains exotic herbs and even a few bug-eating plants.

Going to church has probably never been so varied and so fun!

KEEP IN MIND
While the cathedral is a cool place for kids, it's still a house of worship, so encourage children to be as quiet as church mice in the main church and chapels. If they need to let off steam, take them to the Bishop's Garden, ideal for hide-and-seek.

HEY, KIDS! At the east side of St. Peter's tower, almost at the top, is a stone grotesque of Darth Vader, a model of which is in the Medieval Workshop. A 13-year-old boy won a contest to design a decorative sculpture for the cathedral. Bring binoculars. They make Vader—and a lot of the other gargoyles—easier to spot.

WHEATON REGIONAL PARK

All aboard! A little red replica of an 1863 train chugs along on 10-minute tours through the woods at this park within 10 miles of D.C. But there's more for children here than just choo-choo rides.

Your youngsters can whiz around on a carousel, ride a life-size statue of a camel, or peer over the turrets of a castle, conveniently located in a sandbox that can accommodate a whole class of kids. The playground is packed with bouncing wooden bridges, ladders, swings, mazes, wooden jeeps with bright plastic steering wheels, and straight and spiral slides in all sizes—from less than 6 feet long to more than 60 feet long.

Facilities for sports lovers include hiking trails, an ice rink, tennis courts, baseball fields, and basketball courts. The Brookside Nature Center offers dozens of free and low-cost nature programs throughout the year, including hikes, puppet shows, workshops, and summer camps, but even without a special program, the nature center is a fun place to visit.

EATS FOR KIDS Picnic tables are scattered throughout the park. If you're planning for a crowd, consider renting a picnic shelter (tel. 301/495–2525), where you're guaranteed a dry place to eat, rain or shine. **Wheaton Plaza** (11160 Viers Mill Rd., tel. 301/946–3200), about 3 miles away, has a food court.

KEEP IN MIND If you're closer to the Potomac, you might prefer 500-acre Cabin John Regional Park (7400 Tuckerman La., Rockville, MD, tel. 301/299–0024). Your child can pretend to ride Cinderella's pumpkin coach or watch the Bethesda Big Train baseball team (tel. 301/983–1006) play in a summer league. Facilities here also include a train replica that takes children through the forest and alongside the playground, where kids often wave to the train passengers. Feed trash to the talking pig near the train station.

 2000 Shorefield Rd., Wheaton, MD; nature center 1400 Glenallan Ave.; gardens 1800 Glenallan Ave.

 Free; some attractions charge

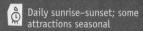 Daily sunrise–sunset; some attractions seasonal

 301/680–3803, 301/946–9071 nature center, 301/949–8230 gardens; www.mc-mncppc.org; www.brooksidegardens.org

 6 mth and up

Kids can check out live snakes, fish, and turtles; play nature games on the computer; and put puzzles together.

Next to the nature center is Brookside Gardens, where formal seasonal displays of bulbs, annuals, and perennials and a sprawling azalea garden flourish outside and seasonal displays and exotic tropicals blossom inside. The garden's annual children's day, usually held on the third or fourth Saturday in September, features sing-alongs, crafts, and games. During the winter, take a stroll through Brookside's Garden of Lights. You won't see Santa or a menorah at this secular presentation, but you will see bears, owls, squirrels, cherry trees, and black-eyed Susans—all lit up brighter than stars to enchant children of all ages.

HEY, KIDS! Try finding the queen bee in the beehive at the Brookside Nature Center. (It's even trickier than finding Waldo because all the bees are moving.) Beekeepers put a dot on her back, and she's slightly bigger than the hundreds of other honeybees swarming around behind glass. You can get within a ½" of them and not get stung. You can also watch the bees move freely between their home in the nature center and the outdoors.

WHITE HOUSE AND VISITOR CENTER

President Dwight Eisenhower called the White House "a living story of past pioneering, struggles, wars, innovations, and a growing America." Children may see this living story with their school or youth group by scheduling a tour through a member of congress. Tours last about 20–25 minutes and take you through the East Room (where Teddy Roosevelt allowed his children to ride a pony), the Green Room, the Blue Room, the Red Room, and the State Dining Room.

Fortunately, there is another place to learn about our country's most famous house—through its Visitor Center. A video of the first lady guiding you through the house continually plays. Check out the pictures of presidents, their families, and their pets. Challenge your child to find the gingerbread house, the pet pony named Macaroni, and the family prankster who ate all the strawberries intended for a state dinner and the gingerbread house.

KEEP IN MIND Take a White House Un-Tour, an unofficial walking tour about the presidential mansion and learn some official but off the wall fun facts, such as how many buckets of paint it takes to coat the White House. Kids can even "become" presidents and learn about the changes—good or bad—they made to the Executive Mansion. Meet at 10:30 AM, Tu–Sa, Memorial Day through Labor Day at the McPherson Square Metrorail Station, "White House" exit (tel. 202/484–1565; www.washingtonwalks.com; $10 adults, $5 kids 12 and under, younger than age 3 free).

1600 Pennsylvania Ave. NW; Visitor
Center, 1450 Pennsylvania Ave. NW.
Metro: Federal Triangle

 Free

T–Sa 7:45–10:30 AM (school and youth
groups only; tours may be canceled
without notice); Visitor Center daily 7–4

202/456–7041 recording, 202/208–1631 voice;
www.whitehouse.gov; www.nps.gov/whho

 5 and up

Kids like presents. So do presidents. Not only can you see some spectacular silver and china (no big deal to kids), you can also find a picture of more creative gifts such as the black and white furry friends from China.

Just as if you were touring the actual White House, you can't bring in any food or drink, even water, with you. But unlike the president's place, the Visitor Center has room to roam and rest (seats and benches), as well as rest rooms and water fountains, which aren't available on the White House tour.

Children can share their opinions with the president by emailing him at president@whitehouse.gov or penning a letter. The president and first lady even have their own zip code: 20500.

EATS FOR KIDS
At **Old Ebbitt Grill** (675 15th St. NW, tel. 202/347–4800), a Washington tradition since 1856, parents like the homemade pasta, and kids like the goodies accompanying their meals. A food hall in the **Shops** (National Place, F and G Sts. between 13th and 14th Sts. NW, tel. 202/662–1200) has everything from greasy fries to gourmet salads.

HEY, KIDS! Visit the information desk at the Visitor Center. You can learn what happened in history on the day you visit and see if any special events are planned. One day a month, a professional actor pretends to be a president or patriot, but any day you can put your own patriotic powers to work by completing the President's Park "On this Spot" Junior Ranger Program brochure.

WOLF TRAP NATIONAL PARK
FOR THE PERFORMING ARTS

Over a stream and through the woods, you'll find a clearing with benches and a stage where the National Park Service sponsors Theatre-in-the-Woods for at least seven weeks every summer. Though this venue is most often associated with adult concerts, as many as 800 people per performance come here to see professional children's performers, such as jugglers, musicians, clowns, and puppeteers. Sometimes a former Harlem Globetrotter shows off his basketball artistry and antics.

Afterward, romping through the park is encouraged. Children (and parents) roll down the grassy hill and picnic in the meadow under shady trees. Sometimes park rangers give impromptu nature tours after the performances. Rangers, who may be college students or teachers, sometimes point out Virginia's state tree (the dogwood) and bird (the cardinal). They may also talk about how the bark and roots of the sassafras tree were used not only to make perfume, soap, and medicine, but also to flavor root beer.

HEY, KIDS! So why is this place called Wolf Trap Farm Park? During Colonial times, this area was farmland, and farmers, who considered wolves a danger to livestock, would reward anyone who trapped the creatures. There haven't been wolves here for ages, but you may spot deer, foxes, or groundhogs.

KEEP IN MIND On Tuesday, Thursday, and Saturday after the 10 o'clock shows, performers stay for about 40 minutes to teach workshops for children 5 and up. Groups of about 35 kids gain insight into the performing arts, learning puppetry, proper clown etiquette, simple ballet techniques, or mime moves. Reservations aren't required for performances, but they're a must for the free workshops.

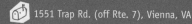 1551 Trap Rd. (off Rte. 7), Vienna, VA

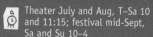 703/255–1860, 703/255–1827 theater, 703/642–0862 festival; www.wolftrap.org

 Theater $4 ages 3 and up; festival $10 ages 13 and up, $8 children 3–12

 Theater July and Aug, T–Sa 10 and 11:15; festival mid-Sept, Sa and Su 10–4

2–11

For one weekend in September, Wolf Trap hosts the International Children's Festival, which features performers, crafts, and music from other countries. If your kids are too young to know about countries, they're probably familiar with streets, especially the one called Sesame. Bob McGrath ("Bob" on *Sesame Street*). Three stages—the Theatre-in-the-Woods, the Meadow Pavilion, and the Filene Center (a covered amphitheater)—feature entertainment from puppet shows to clowns. Kids who want their faces or wrists painted can choose from more than the usual animal or flower—they can select a flag from one of the countries celebrated or a U.S. flag. One of the most popular festival areas is the Arts/Technology Pavilion. In the past, kids have designed roller coasters on computers, interacted with a robot, and danced for video cameras.

Everything except food is included in the price. If it rains, everything moves to tents and the Filene Center. It is hoped that this won't dampen spirits too much.

EATS FOR KIDS No food or drink (except water) is permitted in the theater, because of bees and animals that might want to nibble your lunch. If you bring food, you'll have to keep it securely wrapped during the show. Ten minutes away at the **Rainforest Café** (1961 Chain Bridge Rd., Fairfax, tel. 703/821–1900), in the Tyson's Corner Shopping Center, animated wildlife, waterfalls, and other special effects entertain diners.

extra! extra!

CLASSIC GAMES

"I SEE SOMETHING YOU DON'T SEE AND IT IS BLUE." Stuck for a way to get your youngsters to settle down in a museum? Sit them down on a bench in the middle of a room and play this vintage favorite. The leader gives just one clue—the color—and everybody guesses away.

"I'M GOING TO THE GROCERY..." The first player begins, "I'm going to the grocery and I'm going to buy... " and finishes the sentence with the name of an object, found in grocery stores, that begins with the letter "A." The second player repeats what the first player has said, and adds the name of another item that starts with "B." The third player repeats everything that has been said so far and adds something that begins with "C" and so on through the alphabet. Anyone who skips or misremembers an item is out (or decide up front that you'll give hints to all who need 'em). You can modify the theme depending on where you're going that day, as "I'm going to X and I'm going to see..."

FAMILY ARK Noah had his ark—here's your chance to build your own. It's easy: Just start naming animals and work your way through the alphabet, from antelope to zebra.

PLAY WHILE YOU WAIT

NOT THE GOOFY GAME Have one child name a category. (Some ideas: first names, last names, animals, countries, friends, feelings, foods, hot or cold things, clothing.) Then take turns naming things that fall into that category. You're out if you name something that doesn't belong in the category—or if you can't think of another item to name. When only one person remains, start again. Choose categories depending on where you're going or where you've been—historic topics if you've seen a historic sight, animal topics before or after the zoo, upside-down things if you've been to the circus, and so on. Make the game harder by choosing category items in A-B-C order.

DRUTHERS How do your kids really feel about things? Just ask. "Would you rather eat worms or hamburgers? Hamburgers or candy?" Choose serious and silly topics—and have fun!

BUILD A STORY "Once upon a time there lived..." Finish the sentence and ask the rest of your family, one at a time, to add another sentence or two. Bring a tape recorder along to record the narrative—and you can enjoy your creation again and again.

GOOD TIMES GALORE

WIGGLE & GIGGLE Give your kids a chance to stick out their tongues at you. Start by making a face, then have the next person imitate you and add a gesture of his own—snapping fingers, winking, clapping, sneezing, or the like. The next person mimics the first two and adds a third gesture, and so on.

JUNIOR OPERA During a designated period of time, have your kids sing everything they want to say.

THE QUIET GAME Need a good giggle—or a moment of calm to figure out your route? The driver sets a time limit and everybody must be silent. The last person to make a sound wins.

HIGH FIVES

BEST IN TOWN
Capital Children's Museum
Mount Vernon
National Air and Space Museum
National Museum of Natural History
National Zoo

BEST OUTDOORS
Wheaton Regional Park (gardens and nature center)

WACKIEST
D.C. Ducks

BEST CULTURAL ACTIVITY
National Gallery of Art and Sculpture Garden

NEW & NOTEWORTHY
The City Museum of Washington, D.C.
Crayola Works
International Spy Museum
National Musuem of the American Indian

BEST MUSEUM
National Museum of Natural History

SOMETHING FOR EVERYONE

ART ATTACK
Corcoran Gallery of Art, **57**
Crayola Works, **56**
Hirshhorn Museum and Sculpture Garden, **44**
Made By You, **37**
National Gallery of Art and Sculpture Garden, **30**
National Museum of African Art, **28**
National Museum of Women in the Arts, **23**
Phillips Collection, **17**
Sackler Gallery/Freer Gallery of Art, **14**

CULTURE CLUB
Capital Children's Museum, **63**
The City Museum of Washington, D.C., **60**
National Geographic's Explorers Hall, **29**
National Museum of African Art, **28**
Sackler Gallery/Freer Gallery of Art, **14**

FARMS AND ANIMALS
Claude Moore Colonial Farm at Turkey Run, **59**
Leesburg Animal Park, **39**
National Aquarium, **33**
National Zoo, **21**
Oxon Cove Park, **19**
Rock Creek Park, **16**

GET YOUR BEARINGS
The Castle (Smithsonian Building), **62**
The City Museum of Washington, D.C. **60**
National Building Museum, **32**
National Museum of American History, **27**
National Postal Museum, **22**

GOOD SPORTS
Bowie Baysox Baseball, **66**
East Potomac Park, **51**
Mystics Basketball, **35**
Wheaton Regional Park, **3**

ALL AROUND TOWN

MANY THANKS

This book is dedicated with appreciation to the Smithsonian Institution employees and volunteers, the National Park Service rangers, and all the museum guides, naturalists, and docents who make Washington such an enriching environment for children. On a personal note, I am grateful to my children and their nine cousins, who range in age from 1 to 17, for helping me to witness Washington's wonders through the eyes of children.

—Kathryn McKay

the end.